Messiah of the Masses

To Leah Pace Jeansonne

Messiah of the Masses

Huey P. Long and the Great Depression

Glen Jeansonne
University of Wisconsin—Milwaukee

Edited by Oscar Handlin

An imprint of Addison Wesley Longman, Inc.

New York • Reading, Massachusetts • Menlo Park, California • Harlow, England
Don Mills, Ontario • Sydney • Mexico City • Madrid • Amsterdam

Executive Editor: Bruce Borland
Project Editor: David Nickol
Design Supervisor: Mary Archondes
Production Manager/Assistant: Willie Lane/Sunaina Sehwani
Compositor: Ampersand Graphics, Ltd.
Text and Cover Printer/Binder: Malloy Lithographing, Inc.

Messiah of the Masses: Huey P. Long and the Great Depression
Copyright © 1993 by Addison-Wesley Educational Publishers Inc.

Library of Congress Cataloging-in-Publication Data

Jeansonne, Glen, 1946–
     Messiah of the masses : Huey P. Long and the Great
Depression / Glen Jeansonne.
          p.   cm.
     Includes bibliographical references and index.
     ISBN 0-06-500162-1
     1. Long, Huey Pierce, 1893–1935.   2. Depressions—1929—
United States.   3. Louisiana—Politics and government—
1865–1950.   4. United States—Politics and government—
1933–1945.   5. Legislators—United States—Biography.
6. Governors—Louisiana—Biography.   7. United States.
Congress. Senate—Biography.   I. Title.
E748.L86J43   1993
976.3'06'092—dc20   92-15963
[B]   CIP

12 13 14 15-DOC-01 00 99

Contents

Editor's Preface

Fastidious observers outside the South discounted the significance of the succession of popular leaders who periodically thrust themselves forward in one state or another after Reconstruction. Often such politicians gained local power by claiming to voice the people's grievances; sometimes they had intruded into the national legislature. While their rantings may have won votes, they carried little conviction outside the range of their voices, and they lacked the ability to frame coherent programs even in the interests of their constituents. Judged by the standards of rational statesmanship, they were a bewildering irrelevancy.

Yet judged by the standard of the voters who elected them, these picturesque politicians formed a significant force. Though some used their offices to enrich themselves and betrayed the trust their followers put in them, they attracted loyalty and voted by voicing the genuine grievances of desperate people.

Rural southerners had prospered only in the past shaped by the plantation and slavery. At the opening of the twentieth century, the region's agriculture had not yet recovered from the ravages of Civil War and Reconstruction; and only briefly, during World War I, had it enjoyed a measure of prosperity, before sinking into poverty. Louisiana suffered as much as other states and bore the additional burden of divisions between blacks and whites, rich and poor, French and English, Catholics and Protestants, residents of New Orleans and upcountry farmers. Oil added to the stakes but solved no problems; politics provided a field for contests, not for the adjustment of conflicts.

Huey P. Long entered upon this dismal scene, and from early on scrambled to rise by whatever means came to hand. His family was not wealthy, but neither was it among the poorest in the parish (county). Still, the young Huey knew what poverty was and determined to rise above it. Impatient with schooling, he nevertheless glimpsed the importance of education and later would do what he could to further it in the state. Meanwhile he could not waste time on learning. Ruthless, he also knew the utility of law, not as an instrument of justice but as a means toward grasping power. His career throws valuable light upon the background of the Great Depression and upon the changing features of modern America.

Oscar Handlin

Author's Preface

Based upon a lifetime in Louisiana, four previous books dealing with Louisiana's history, and the teaching of Louisiana history on the college level, I have felt for many years that Huey Long was a misunderstood figure. Too often he has been studied out of context, either by parochial Louisianans or by non-Louisianans who lacked an appreciation of the state's political complexities. Both the Long and the anti-Long factions have been stereotyped and some facile generalizations by previous biographers have no basis in fact.

Long operated in different contexts nationally and locally. He did not do in Louisiana what he preached nationally; hence, the Louisiana audience and the national audience each saw only a part of the picture. Yet one without the other is incomplete. The constituents he embraced and intended to attract nationally were not identical to those in Louisiana, nor were the origins of his state and national followings identical. Long's appeal, on both levels, was a product of his times, and it changed over time. He appeared on the Louisiana scene prior to the Great Depression promising to cut state spending and eliminate waste, duplication, and payroll padding, then preceded to accelerate them. In planning to run for national office, his emphasis shifted. Minor themes became major themes. His attitude toward race changed somewhat. Most politicians who rise from local to national prominence experience a similar evolution.

I do not believe Long was entirely sincere, but neither was he wholly hypocritical. I doubt that many major politicians are entirely sincere, an attitude exacerbated in Long by the cynicism of Louisiana's political environment. Neither do I believe Long was purely a saint or purely a sinner, although I do believe he always put his own interests first.

Writing for a national audience, I have emphasized Long's national career more than if I had written specifically for a Louisiana audience. Although the series format precludes footnotes, I would be happy to furnish my sources to those interested. Much of this study is derived from primary sources, some never used previously in exactly the same manner. Moreover, I believe previous scholars have overlooked some revealing details available all along.

I hope I have provided an interpretation that is both fresh and fair, and one that is forthright and unafraid to advance a thesis, without being dogmatic. It is part orthodox, part unorthodox. Perhaps if it arouses mixed feelings among both Long's partisans and his critics, it is because Long inspires mixed feelings within the author. He was a man of great abilities and tragic flaws.

I do not think one can place Long adequately in historical context by stopping abruptly at his death. Both his sins and his accomplishments endured and were altered and obscured by time. Longism outlived Huey Long in Louisiana and both locally, and nationally his life and death had repercussions beyond his lifetime. Many people have contributed to this book but few would agree with everything I say. I am grateful for the opportunity to say it.

Glen Jeansonne

Acknowledgments

I am grateful to Michael Gauger, who edited and indexed the manuscript; to Charlotte Gallagher, who edited the manuscript; and to Kari Frederickson, who helped with the research and proofreading. The entire staff of the Louisiana State University Library was most helpful. William Ivy Hair permitted me to read his manuscript on Long prior to publication. Bruce Borland of HarperCollins and Oscar Handlin also deserve my gratitude. My wife, Sharon Pace Jeansonne, critically read the manuscript, and she and my daughters, Leah and Hannah, provided a nurturing environment.

Glen Jeansonne

Messiah of the Masses

CHAPTER ONE

The Young Man

❖
❖

Huey Long reflected the complexity of his native state, a place of swamps and pine trees, snakes and alligators, gentle hills and steamy heat, breathtaking beauty and hopeless poverty. Its population was diverse, its economy wretchedly poor but potentially rich, its infrastructure underdeveloped, its people cynical about politics. Louisianans would remain poor, although after Huey Long they would no longer be hopeless but would pursue for generations the utopia he had promised but not provided. His accomplishments were self-inflated, yet he generated a revolution in expectations with the promise that every man could become a king. Most visible in 1935 was the glitter of the promise, not the hard facts.

Remote from markets, lacking an industrial base and adequate transportation, Louisiana remained predominantly rural. The rural population might have been even higher were it not for the existence of New Orleans, the largest city in the South during Long's lifetime. New Orleans represented an urban outpost surrounded by a rural hinterland, and thus had enormous ramifications for Louisiana's politics.

If Louisiana's white population was indigent, its black population, declining as many left the state for better jobs and more freedom, was economically prostrate. Few blacks lived or worked in cities, and the vast majority earned their living on farms. Some worked as agricultural laborers, three-fourths of whom earned less than one dollar a day as late as 1937. The only significant areas of employment for blacks outside farming was with the Standard Oil Company in Baton Rouge and as long-shoremen at the port of New Orleans. In 1927 Standard Oil employed 1,757 blacks, one-third of its labor force; 4,440 blacks worked as longshoremen. Louisiana State University was a Jim Crow institution and there were few alternatives available to blacks who wanted a higher education. Only 48 blacks gradu-ated from college in Louisiana in 1930.

Blacks had no voice in state politics. Since the adoption of the Constitution in 1898, and subsequent amendments, they had been disenfranchised by the white primary, poll tax, and literacy test. White registrars routinely disqualified blacks who had the temerity to attempt to register on the grounds that they did not "understand" the state or federal constitutions although many white registrars who administered such tests were them-selves functional illiterates. Even the tiny minority of blacks who qualified could vote only in general elections, rendered meaningless because Republicans rarely challenged Demo-crats, and never won.

Louisiana, an atypical southern state, was an anomaly in the United States. Ethnically, geographically, economically, and religiously, its complexity was baffling. Settled by the French, the Spanish, the English, and other peoples during different periods, it remained multilingual, a potpourri of ethnic groups, partly segregated by geography.

In 1920 almost 60 percent of church members were Roman Catholics; 54 of the 64 parishes (counties) were more than two-thirds Catholic or more than two-thirds Protestant, mostly Bap-tists and Methodists.

South Louisiana, colonized by France and Spain, was over-whelmingly Catholic. Blessed by oil deposits and fertile delta soil, the south was the most prosperous and populous part of the state. South Louisiana had its squalid side as well—gam-bling, drinking, dancing, and prostitution were popular, espe-cially in New Orleans, where it took federal prohibition agent Isadore Einstein only 37 seconds to find a drink. A port city and international trading center with a large foreign population, with concentrated wealth beside abject poverty, with fine homes, urban sprawl, and ghetto squalor, the metropolis differed dramatically from the rest of the state.

Monolithically Protestant, stridently fundamentalist, the northern parishes had much in common with neighboring Arkansas and Mississippi.

Democracy never flourished in Louisiana, whose entire colonial history was characterized by power struggles among public officials, nationalities, and races. Unlike the British colonies, Louisiana had no representative assembly, allowing the governor to be all the more powerful.

Race transcended class. Although sometimes interpreted as a false issue by which rich whites oppressed poor whites, the exclusion of blacks from the political process was really an issue on which all classes of white voters agreed. Historians have sometimes assumed blacks were disenfranchised to cement the Bourbons in power. In reality it was just the opposite. Disenfranchisement weakened the Bourbons because blacks customarily were counted as having voted for the conservative Democratic candidates—regardless of how they actually voted and even if they did not vote.

Louisiana, and particularly Long's part of the state, was influenced by Populism. The Populists, chiefly southern and western farmers, sought governmental intervention in the economy to relieve their financial distress during the depression of the early 1890s. Long never mentioned Populism in his speeches, nor did any Long ever vote for a Populist; nonetheless, there are some similarities between the Populist platform and Huey Long's own program. Moreover, Long appealed to much the same constituency that the Populists represented and Longism and Populism were both rural and antimodern.

Although Populism was provoked by hard times and many of the grievances were economic, not every impoverished farmer became a Populist and those who did were not necessarily poorer than those who did not. Environmental factors motivated many Populists. Populism peaked when America was becoming increasingly urban and industrial, leaving the Populists bewildered by a society that was changing more rapidly than they could adapt. Defensive about their naïveté, they stood on the periphery, literally and figuratively, making scapegoats of the plutocracy and proposing vague panaceas.

Although Populism and Longism evinced reactionary characteristics their critique of society was not irrelevant. Both groups viewed the world from a perspective that was anti-modern. Differences in language, temperament, recreational inclinations, and work ethics slowed the development of a modern industrial economy in Louisiana. The state's bountiful natural resources also worked to its disadvantage, particularly because Louisiana lacked the local capital to develop them. A state with fertile soil and numerous minerals was conducive to the development of an economy based on agriculture and the extraction of raw materials. Louisiana flourished in the pre-industrial economy of the antebellum South, but when the basis of the economy was destroyed by the abolition of slavery, the state had no industry to compensate. Louisiana politicians, a rather unimaginative group, did not create the situation, they merely reflected it.

Populism and Longism appealed to provincial people. Long's neo-Populism fed upon isolation and alienation from mainstream culture. His program, oratory, and mannerisms were rural. Long intuitively distrusted modernization and the consolidation of business and capital. His tenacity and drive were fueled by his own alienation. By defeating the "better" element he also gratified his constituents.

Long became governor shortly before the Great Depression, but Louisiana was already in a depression, a field awaiting tilling by an economic messiah. The Depression not only accentuated Long's appeal in Louisiana, it inspired a national following.

There was little in Longism that was revolutionary. To a Californian, a Wisconsinite, or a Mississippian, it would not have seemed particularly original to propose giving free schoolbooks. Students in those states and in 38 others already had them. Yet to rural Louisianans, the idea seemed revolutionary. They believed, justifiably, that previous politicians had ignored them.

Although they were neither unusually reactionary nor conspicuously venal, Louisiana's leaders in the immediate pre-Long era lacked imagination and magnetism. They constituted a desert barren of new ideas, not an autocracy of wealth and privilege. Nor was the state dominated by an industrial elite; on the contrary, it lacked industry and its elite was more culturally than politically inclined. Long rose to power attacking millionaires, but at the time he became governor there was not a single person in Louisiana earning a millionaire's income and as late as 1930 there was only one person with an income greater than $500,000. Standard Oil, Long's nemesis, did not dictate state politics. A national corporation that could have been regulated effectively only at the national level, Standard protected its interests, as did other economic entities, but it avoided, rather than provoked, political brawls.

What characterized Louisiana politics was not a shadowy plutocracy but virtual chaos. Like other rural southern states its politics were not monolithic and rigidly orchestrated but decentralized. Organization requires money, leadership, and ideology. Louisiana's politicians before Long lacked all three. There was one exception—and it was a mammoth exception—New Orleans. It possessed the only substantial concentration of wealth in the state and the only effective political machine in the South, the Old Regulars, also called the Choctaws or, simply, the Regulars. The Old Regulars flourished on patronage and provided social services that the state did not. Like northern city machines, they ran the city corruptly and inefficiently, albeit with some humaneness.

One might think that with 20 percent of the state's population, New Orleans controlled state politics. Just the reverse was true. Rarely could a New Orleanian win the governorship, rarer yet a Catholic New Orleanian. The Regulars could mobilize a respectable majority for a hometown candidate, although the rural antipathy to Catholics and city slickers made such candidacies futile. Consequently the machine seldom attempted to dictate a governor and usually was content to endorse one who would practice benign neglect. Indeed, neglect, not upper-class or corporate oppression, characterized state politics.

The sin of Louisiana's pre-Long governors was indifference. They presided over a state they perceived to be placid but was, in fact, ready to erupt. Anyone should have realized that there were more rural voters than urban ones, more poor ones than rich ones, and that anyone who could unite them would achieve political domination.

Huey Long's accomplishment in Louisiana was monumental, if misunderstood. What he did was not to replace parochial issues with economic theories, nor to impose liberalism in a conservative backwater. Instead, he imposed order upon chaos. If Congress moves at the pace of a turtle, Louisiana's legislature before Long moved at the pace of a snail. Under Long, it became hyperactive. By 1934 Longite bills were spewing out of the Legislature at the rate of one bill every two minutes. It was as if Henry Ford had brought the assembly line to the legislative process. The activity of Congress during Franklin Roosevelt's first 100 days was pedestrian compared to the Louisiana legislature in 1934 and 1935.

Long's state opponents were ineffective not because they were dogmatic conservatives, but because they were rudderless. None of them possessed his mass appeal or organizational ability. Most had never dealt with anyone such as Huey, who did not play by the rules. Consistently outwitted, they became demoralized.

Long was born August 30, 1893, in Winnfield, the seat of Winn Parish, in northeastern Louisiana. Winn was one of the least fertile areas in Louisiana. Settled late, after choicer land had been occupied, it was one of the last parishes created. Winn's chief resource was timber; longleaf pine became the basis of sawmills and the manufacture of plywood, glue, and railroad ties. The parish also produced livestock, cotton, salt, oil, and gas. The lumber mills moved in around 1900, and the land was soon stripped of trees, leaving the soil to bake in the sun and erode from the rain.

Poor, provincial Winnfield was unusually isolated even for Louisiana, its thin red soil and rolling hills not conducive to plantation agriculture. About one in four families owned slaves before the Civil War, and the 1,300 slaves constituted about one-third of the population. (When Long was born the parish was 14 percent black.) Winn remained out of the mainstream. Its delegate to the Louisiana Convention of 1861 voted against secession, but subsequently joined the Confederate army and raised three companies of troops.

In the 1880s Winn became one of the first parishes to participate in the Farmers' Alliance, and in 1890 it was the birthplace of Louisiana's Populist Party. Populist gubernatorial candidates carried Winn in 1892 and 1896; in the latter year the party's candidate was a Winnfield native. In the first years of the 1900s Winn was even tempted by Socialism; Eugene V. Debs polled 36 percent of the parish vote for president in 1912, his highest percentage in the state. Rebellion and alienation characterized Winn, where the indigent farmers had little to lose by change and rebelled against the status quo, be it conservative or liberal. Huey was not popular in his birthplace and during his political career polled a smaller percentage of the Winnfield vote than he did in other towns in north Louisiana.

Winnfield was a quiet community during Long's boyhood. In 1910 its population was 2,900, and it lacked municipal water and electricity. Its business district was comprised of two hotels, a lumber mill, and seven other buildings. A fire that destroyed parish records in the nineteenth century created a thriving business for attorneys, who traced lost deeds.

Huey was named after his father, Hugh Pierce Long, who outlived him. The family had settled in Maryland, migrated to Ohio, then moved to Mississippi. Huey's grandfather came to Louisiana in 1859, and his father settled in Winnfield in 1892 with six children. Four more children were born in Winnfield, including Huey; one died in infancy.

Huey's father was a man of intelligence and magnetism. Standing nearly 6 feet tall and extremely thin, he had a loud voice and loved to talk, but was gentle, even weak. Hugh had only a rudimentary education, having dropped out of elementary school. He took his father's struggling farm and turned a profit after changing from cotton to livestock. When Hugh moved to Winnfield he purchased 320 acres of uncleared farmland and commenced moderately successful operations. He sold part of his property for a handsome profit when the

Arkansas Southern Railroad built a line through Winnfield in 1901. With the railroad's arrival, Winn and the Longs prospered. When the town expanded Hugh subdivided some of his property and sold lots to businessmen.

Huey Long was born in a large, commodious log cabin on his father's farm. The following year the Longs moved to a better dwelling and in 1907 Hugh built one of the larger houses in Winnfield, with 16 rooms, electric lights, indoor plumbing, high ceilings, and large verandas. In 1910 an article in a Winnfield paper stated, "Few, if any, have greater proprietary interests at stake in our town than Mr. [Hugh] Long," and one of his neighbors described the Longs as being part "of the upper crust." When family fortunes peaked, they even employed a black servant. Huey later exaggerated the poverty of his childhood to enhance his appeal to constituents and to make his achievements appear more impressive. His siblings thought his depiction of their impoverishment demeaning. "He made us all so mad," one sister wrote. "He warped things for political reasons." Huey's sisters became furious when he said on the Senate floor in 1935, "My brothers and sisters, my uncles and aunts, my relatives and friends, are starving to death." His older brother, Julius, wrote in 1933, "He wanted it to appear that all of us, except him, are an insignificant, worthless bunch."

Despite his scant education, Hugh Long was impressive, dominating every conversation. He was a fine public speaker, "better and wittier than any of his sons," Huey's sister Lucille said, yet his political aspirations went nowhere. In 1900 he finished a distant third in a three-way race for the state Senate. In 1910 he finished sixth in a campaign for five aldermen. Huey was embarrassed by his father's political failures; he thought people might consider the Longs losers. He was never close to his father, whom he considered weak, an idle talker who wasted his life, and resented the need to support his father in old age. He wrote to his brother, George, who asked him to help Hugh purchase land to farm: "If the old man can't make it on what he has we will just have to let [him] go. It may be the best thing any way not to put out any more money. Let him piddle around on what he already has." The animosity appeared mutual. In 1932 when Hugh sat on the platform at an anti-Huey rally and heard a speaker describe Huey as a man who had no feeling for his family, he "stamped his feet in approval."

Huey's mother Caledonia was more forceful than her husband and more intelligent. Callie, like Hugh, was slender, standing 5' 5" and weighing less than 100 pounds. Unlike Hugh she possessed a disciplined mind. Self-educated, she had a near-photographic memory. She enforced family discipline but her attempts to discipline Huey were ineffective. Huey resisted authority and could not tolerate anyone who told him what to do. "He ain't never been nothing but a pesterance to her," one neighbor said of Huey and his mother. Callie died in 1913, at 52, of typhoid; Huey was 20.

Callie was more pious than Hugh, and although he avoided church services, she attended and compelled her children to go. The Longs appeared at the First Baptist Church of Winnfield on Sunday mornings, Sunday evenings, and at Wednesday night prayer meetings. They also attended weddings and funerals. Huey enjoyed singing, experienced "salvation," and was baptized in a neighbor's fishpond. He considered becoming a minister, aware that the preacher was the center of attention. But church bored him and, as a teenager, he began using profanity, chewing tobacco, smoking, and drinking. As an adult, he violated most of the biblical commandments, yet Long, who seldom thought about a supreme being, retained an almost superstitious respect for the mystical and tithed, hedging his bets, in case there was a hell. One of his lieutenants observed that although Huey did not have any religious prejudices, he did not have any religion either. George Wallace, who drafted legislation for Long, said he was not a religious man. Long peppered his speeches with inaccurate biblical quotations to impress rural audiences, which his brother Julius thought hypocritical. "A more irreligious, profane man I have never known," Julius wrote. "If he has any respect for any religion I have never known it. I doubt that he has been to church half a dozen times in five years."

Huey clashed with his siblings. Notoriously contentious, the Long children included four brothers and five sisters, all highly intelligent. Julius, Huey, and Earl became attorneys and George a dentist. The girls received college degrees in education and one became a professor. Huey considered himself intellectually superior to his siblings, but they condemned his egotism.

Julius, 14 years older than Huey, considered himself Huey's mentor. As adults, though, they became bitter enemies. In 1933 Julius termed Huey "a disgrace to the state of Louisiana" and complained, "as a child he was always disagreeable among his sisters and brothers." Julius concluded that political success came too easily to Huey and that he did not appreciate the sacrifices his family had made for him.

Julius became the family's first attorney. He received a bachelor's degree from what is now Louisiana Tech University, then a law degree from Tulane University after one year of study, and in 1912 was elected district attorney for Winn and Jackson parishes. He believed that Huey, with proper guidance, could earn respect for the Longs and enhance their social status. He failed, however, to tame his younger brother's impudence.

Huey had a love–hate relationship with his youngest brother, Earl. As children they were close, slept in the same bedroom and played together. Slower mentally but stronger physically, Earl did not mind when Huey insulted playmates then fled, leaving the fighting to his brother. Earl was even more successful than Huey in state politics, serving three terms as governor, but intellectually, Huey outclassed him. "Earl is to Huey as a breeze is to a typhoon," said a man who knew both. Earl was less pretentious than Huey and enjoyed chatting, unlike Huey, who considered casual conversation wasteful. Earl had the personal touch Huey lacked; people were awed by Huey yet liked Earl better. Huey disliked dirt and rarely worked on his father's farm. Earl, though, returned to his farm at every opportunity. A shrewd political strategist, Earl served as Huey's "bagman" during his impeachment trial, dispensed patronage, and conceived the "deduct" system of financing the Long machine by extorting contributions from state employees. "Maybe I ain't as great a genius, but I got more horse sense," Earl said.

Huey had less contact with George ("Shan"), the second oldest boy. A hefty six-footer, more relaxed than his siblings, Shan received a degree in dentistry from the University of Kentucky and practiced in Shawnee, Oklahoma, where he earned a modest fortune and was elected to the legislature. After Huey's death he returned to Louisiana and ran three unsuccessful campaigns for Congress before winning in 1952. He served until his death in 1958. Huey's relationship with his sisters was more distant and he seldom spoke about them.

Huey was the eighth of the nine Long children who lived to maturity; only Earl was younger. His parents and siblings knew there was something different about the hyperactive and intensely curious Huey. "He was the most restless one, the most enterprising one," Hugh said. He walked at just nine months and when he was older, he never slowed down. Huey ran a mile from elementary school to his home at noon so he could bolt down lunch, then get back before those who had carried their lunch were finished eating. He kept a messy room at home and was habitually late for meals. He ran away twice before adolescence yet never got far.

Huey's teachers had little luck disciplining him. Although bright, he rarely studied, made mediocre grades, and, as he grew older, showed contempt for his teachers. He thought he knew so much that there was nothing they could teach him. He skipped the seventh grade on his own volition; he simply showed up in the eighth-grade classroom when the term began.

Huey avoided rough sports and would not play softball unless he could pitch. He badly wanted to win every competition and trounce the opposition. He craved attention and insisted on being the focal point of every activity, a competitive spirit he retained all his life. "Huey had to be the top dog or it was no go," observed one of his political associates.

A Winnfield High School classmate had similar impressions. Long once snatched a newspaper the other student was reading, which carried an article about the governor's Thanksgiving proclamation. Huey read it aloud, substituting his name for the governor's; from then on this classmate called him "Governor." Always brash, Huey signed his schoolbooks

"Hon. Huey P. Long," and invited a young woman to kiss him so that "some day you will be able to say you've kissed the famous Huey Long." Julius considered his younger brother moody and mercurial. "In the twinkling of an eye he can be either wet or dry, hot or cold, for or against."

After he developed intellectual pretensions, Long claimed to have read history and biography as a child. Actually, he rarely read entire books. Neither the town nor the school had a library, but Callie owned some books and Huey read books Julius brought home from college. He loved biographies of Napoleon, Julius Caesar, and Frederick the Great, comparing himself to Frederick, "the greatest son of a bitch who ever lived!" He also enjoyed *The Count of Monte Cristo* and read it repeatedly. "That man in that book knew how to hate," he observed, "and until you learn how to hate you'll never get anywhere in this world." Huey's favorite historian was John Clark Ridpath, who wrote a popular history of the world. It was the only history book he remembered; as a senator he kept it in his office library, and he quoted from it in speeches.

Huey, who had a near-photographic memory, memorized long passages that he quoted verbatim to impress people. However, his memory was highly selective; unless something struck him or had some practical value, he forgot it. He had no inclination toward science or mathematics and read neither philosophy nor religion, except for the Bible. Callie encouraged her children to read, although she compelled them only to read the Bible. After adolescence, Huey lacked the time to read and as an adult read little except newspapers and magazines.

Ridpath and the romantic novels of Victor Hugo and Sir Walter Scott provided Huey with a distorted view of the world. Huey always retained a romantic element to his personality. He relied on impressions and intuition rather than diligent study. "Huey didn't know U.S. history, not as much as I knew," one acquaintance remarked. Though possessing a brilliant mind, Huey was too impatient to observe accuracy. For example, he told a friend that in the War of 1812 the British had "whipped the whole United States except Louisiana, which then saved America from surrender." He did not know that the Battle of

New Orleans had been fought after a peace treaty had already been signed.

Huey might have pretended to read because he wanted to avoid work. "Mama never disturbed a child as long as he was reading, or pretending to read—she would call one that wasn't reading to do the job at hand," Lottie said. Huey, in fact, avoided physical labor. He later claimed to sympathize with the working class, because he had toiled as a youth, but he "never did a hard day's work in his life," Julius remarked. Although Huey rarely helped his father on the farm, he did attempt to earn money at odd jobs. He did a little cotton picking until his employer caught him stuffing a watermelon into his sack to increase the weight. During the summer of 1906, when he was 12, Huey drove a bakery wagon for $3 a week. The following summer he worked as a waterboy for bricklayers building the Winnfield Hotel but quit after a brick fell on his head. At 13 he learned to set type and thereafter worked for two local newspapers, for which he also wrote stories. When setting type he stretched his own articles because he was paid by the inch. Long opportunistically accepted jobs that minimized physical labor. He became adept at those that required speaking skills and all the professions he considered were those in which communication was paramount: the ministry, journalism, sales, law, and politics. He decided to become a politician relatively early because it would enable him to utilize his skills and gratify his need for attention.

Huey learned that he possessed a talent for selling. For several summers he and his best friend, Harley Bozeman, worked on consignment for a book dealer, peddling everything from Bibles to cheap paperbacks in Winn and neighboring parishes. It was a stern test of his ability—if he could sell books in rural Louisiana, he could sell anything. Long found the task much more exciting than schoolwork.

At 15 he and Bozeman were chosen by parish leaders to debate a Socialist speaker. As a fledgling capitalist Long had no sympathy for socialism nor much knowledge of it. He and Bozeman were somewhat humiliated by their better-educated adult opponents and the Socialist candidate for president won a large vote in Winn Parish in the next election. Huey's taste of debate, however, whetted his appetite. As a high school junior he participated in the state literary rally at Louisiana State University in Baton Rouge but did not place. He returned the following year, placed third, and claimed that the judges had cheated him. He stayed overnight in Baton Rouge at the home of Mrs. T. H. Harris, whose husband was the state superintendent of education. Before returning to Winnfield he told her: "Mrs. Harris, you have been mighty good to me, and when I get to be Governor, United States Senator, and President of the United States, I am going to do something for you. I am on my way and will not be stopped by a committee of ignorant professors."

Huey fell in love with LSU and wanted to matriculate there. His prize for placing third in debate was a partial scholarship, but to enroll he would have to graduate from high school, a formidable obstacle because he hated the principal and the feeling was mutual. Huey, Bozeman, and some others created a club that attempted to dictate policy to the principal, who promptly expelled them and would allow them to graduate only after an additional year of study. A bitter Huey left school without a diploma in 1910. Bozeman had obtained a job as a traveling salesman in northeastern Louisiana selling a cottonseed cooking oil called Cottolene, and persuaded his boss to hire Huey. One month shy of his seventeenth birthday, Huey's first full-time job allowed him to travel beyond Winn Parish. His starting salary was $19 a week. Huey would work on the road for the next four years, and although he ended up no richer than he was when he started, he laid the foundation for his political career. Selling taught him much about his future constituents and about himself. He found his love of talking a priceless asset. He also learned that he could establish rapport with country people by asking them personal questions and pretending to be interested in their replies. Traveling by buggy, train, and on foot, he stayed overnight with farmers rather than in hotels. He accumulated a list of acquaintances, some filed on note cards, others in his memory. Long generated a large volume of sales, but he also exceeded his expense account and was insubordinate. He appeared more interested in promoting himself than in selling the product.

Long had no intention of making selling a career. He learned to cook and demonstrated recipes that utilized Cottolene. He quoted biblical prohibitions against pork and told farm wives that the lard they used was condemned by the Bible, while Cottolene was made from cottonseed oil. Long was modestly successful, but he soon concluded that he would not become rich by selling Cottolene. However, he did not want to go back to Winnfield High and the teachers and the principal did not want him.

Long returned to school in January 1911, enrolling in Byrd High School in Shreveport. On his first day he announced, "Class, I'm Huey P. Long from Winnfield and I'm here to stay!" When the chemistry teacher asked for an example of a chemical compound, Huey launched a sales pitch for Cottolene. At recess, he delivered orations. He also worked as a clerk for a plumber and skipped many classes. At a school party he met an attractive young woman named Rose McConnell, who did not understand the brash country upstart. On the one hand she was attracted by his glibness; on the other she was repelled by his arrogance. One trait puzzled her: Huey spent much of his time dashing off letters to politicians, particularly U.S. Senators. When she asked him why he was wasting his time, he told her that some day he would be a Senator and then when he got to Washington he wanted the people there to know him.

During the summer of 1911 Long resumed his position as a traveling salesman for Cottolene. One of his promotional schemes was to conduct baking contests with cakes made from the shortening. Huey served as judge in the Shreveport competition that Rose McConnell, a poor cook, entered. Dubious, Huey asked Rose for a date to prove she had made the cake, then diplomatically, he awarded prizes both to Rose and to her mother. Rose was 15 months older than Huey and after graduating from Byrd High School had obtained a secretarial job. Huey considered her the most beautiful woman he had ever met and decided to marry her. Temperamentally she was quite different from Huey: quiet, shy, calm, and tactful. They had in common a love of music, although neither had training. Everyone, including Rose, thought the couple too young to marry and she rebuffed Huey's proposals for two-and-a-half years. Huey feared he might lose her to another suitor.

Long's job selling Cottolene did not last; in November Huey's employer announced that it was terminating door-to-door sales in north Louisiana. Bozeman then helped Huey to find a position selling wholesale meats for the Houston Packing Company. Huey so impressed the employer that he made Long sales manager for Arkansas. Based in Little Rock, Huey supervised a large number of salesmen though he was not yet 18. There Long attended the political rallies of U.S. Senator Jeff Davis, whose fiery, populistic oratory he never forgot. He also traveled to Mississippi to hear speeches by Governor Theodore Bilbo and U. S. Senator John Sharp Williams.

After only a few months Huey was promoted to manager of a new sales territory that included northern Mississippi and western Tennessee, with headquarters in Memphis. Huey's reputation as a selling wizard increased, but not as fast as his expenses. He lived in the best hotels and ate at the finer restaurants, charging everything to the company, which eventually decided he was losing more money than he was taking in and dismissed him. Huey ran out of money, was ejected from his boarding house, and slept on park benches and at Salvation Army shelters.

Callie, concerned that Huey was wild and was drinking heavily, persuaded him to accept a brother's loan so that he could attend Oklahoma Baptist University in Shawnee. She still believed Huey had the talent to become a Baptist minister. Huey, unemployed, accepted the invitation and money and traveled to Shawnee, where he pretended to enroll. At the end of the fall semester he told his brother he did not have the temperament of a minister and would like to enter law school at the University of Oklahoma.

Huey had talked frequently about becoming an attorney but rarely stuck with anything for more than a few months. His brother believed Huey had potential if his intellect and energy could be harnessed and gave him $100 to begin the second semester. Between the fall and spring semesters, though, Huey went to Kansas City, where he frequented casinos. He lost the entire $100 at roulette and found himself without food, shelter, or transportation, until his brother sent him another $75.

Huey began law classes in January 1912, and remained until the end of the spring semester in May. He studied little, gambled, and sold groceries for the W. K. Dawson Company. If his study was desultory, his prowess at dice and poker improved and he won consistently. Between his salary from Dawson, his winnings at gambling, and contributions from his brother, he lived comfortably.

Long's initial interest in law school soured when he realized that a degree would require study and discipline. More interested in campus politics than classwork, he organized a club supporting Champ Clark of Missouri for the Democratic nomination for president in 1912. The nomination went instead to Woodrow Wilson, whom Huey supported in the general election.

When Huey received his grades, he had earned three C's and an incomplete. Four months had disillusioned him with legal studies. "I didn't learn much law there," Huey said, looking back on his experience in Oklahoma. "Too much excitement, all those gambling houses and everything."

In the spring of 1912 Bozeman helped Huey to obtain a job with the Faultless Starch Company and within a few months Long rose to the position of regional sales manager, headquartered in Memphis. One of the salesmen he hired to work under him was his brother, Earl, who proved nearly as persuasive at selling as Huey.

During the Christmas vacation in 1912 Long returned to Shreveport to visit Rose. Huey was arrested for disturbing the peace and carrying a concealed weapon in an area frequented by prostitutes. Julius and Bozeman rescued Huey from jail; they posted a $150 bond and Julius used his influence to get the charges dropped.

While in Shreveport, Huey proposed again to Rose and she once more deferred a decision. She feared Huey's instability and doubted his ability to make a living. Moreover, Huey was mercurial in his devotion. He bought her a small diamond ring but asked her to return it so he could give it to someone else. Later, he returned and said she could have it after all; the other woman was less attractive than he had thought. The Long and McConnell families were firmly against the match. Huey's mother still believed he was too young to marry and sent Bozeman to Shreveport to try to convince Rose that Huey was immature.

Rose resented Huey's total domination when they were together. She later said she never argued with Huey because it was useless—he would pout until he got his way. Huey was also jealous and would not permit her to enjoy parties. He thought it unfeminine to drink, and if he saw her holding a drink at a party he would race across the room and take it away. Still, he possessed undeniable charm and he was persistent. He called and wrote Rose constantly from Memphis and visited at every opportunity. He told Rose he would have enough money to marry her if he sold an entire carload of starch in Texas. He sold the starch and convinced Rose that he would be an adequate provider. Since the McConnells and Longs considered the marriage unwise, and because Huey was in a hurry, he and Rose were married in a small ceremony in Memphis on April 12, 1913. Less solvent than he pretended, he had to borrow $10 from Rose to pay the minister. The newlyweds moved into a tiny apartment, hoping to find more comfortable quarters when Huey's income increased. Unfortunately, just the opposite happened. In October Huey received two jolts: His mother died and he lost his job. Huey expressed no public remorse over Callie's death, yet he had sufficient reason to become depressed. His life was not working out the way he had planned.

Long remained with the Faultless Starch Company for a few months, but instead of running an office he became a traveling salesman in north Louisiana at a reduced salary. Huey and Rose did not even have a residence of their own. As Huey was constantly away, Rose lived with the Long family in Winnfield or with her parents in Shreveport. In the spring of 1914 Faultless Starch laid Huey off. He obtained another position, peddling patent medicines for the Chattanooga Medicine

Company, a job he kept only a short time before he was fired.

Huey had reached a crossroads. In four years of selling he had lost four jobs. Julius and Rose begged Huey to reconsider law and to resume his studies; they wanted him to attend Tulane University in New Orleans and study hard because he had a family to support. Julius had a thriving practice in Winnfield and had been elected district attorney. He needed a partner and if Huey passed the bar exam he could join Julius's firm. Both Huey and Julius knew that Huey had neither the money nor the patience to attend school for three years and earn a law degree. However, a degree was not necessary for admittance to the bar. Most Louisiana attorneys, rather than obtaining law degrees, studied under an established lawyer, then took selected courses at a university to fill gaps in their knowledge. Julius tutored Huey for several months, provided him with a list of courses to take, and offered to lend him some money. Huey accepted, borrowing $400 from Julius and $250 from State Senator S. J. Harper, whom he referred to as "my one great friend in Winnfield."

Huey should have had enough money to live adequately for at least a year. Huey and Rose moved into a two-room apartment near the university. Rose did not seek a job but instead helped Huey with his studies; he dictated summaries of books, she typed them, and Huey memorized them. Huey registered late for the fall semester as a special student and remained at Tulane through the end of the spring semester in May. His flirtation with poverty had not robbed him of self-confidence; he was outspoken and badgered professors with questions. When one professor lectured on the Louisiana Code, Long piped up that he did not know what he was talking about and the professor promptly ejected him from the course.

For someone living on borrowed money with limited free time, Huey dissipated his energies. He was rejected after trying out for the debate team; the coach told him he talked too loudly and flailed his arms wildly. Huey also sat in on some political science courses because the subject interested him.

In his autobiography Long claimed he studied so much that his weight dropped from 150 pounds to 112. He was compulsive rather than consistently diligent, however, and might study 16 hours one day and not at all the next. His haphazard attendance was reflected in poor grades. He completed only two courses, earning an 83 in one and a 75 in the other; failed two courses; and was absent for the final exam in four others. His transcript shows that he took fewer than one-third of the courses required and received passing grades on only one-twelfth of the necessary work.

Long never intended to remain at Tulane the entire three years or to become a candidate for a degree. By May he felt ready to take the bar exam, which was not administered until June. Knowing that special oral exams could be given at any time by a panel of attorneys with the permission of the state Supreme Court, Long convinced the chief justice that he was needy and deserving of a special exam. He ignored the law requiring attorneys practicing in Winn Parish, where he intended to work, to take the exam in Shreveport. Long managed to bluff his way through the exam, using his quick wit to conceal gaps in knowledge and his prodigious memory to impress the committee. When George Terriberry, an expert in admiralty law, asked Long what he knew about it, Huey replied that he knew nothing. What would he do then, if he were offered an admiralty case? Long replied that he would associate with Terriberry and split the fee.

The examination was perfunctory and Long passed easily. At the age of 21 he was an attorney. He had already crammed an enormous amount of activity into a short life, and was on the threshold of an amazing career.

CHAPTER TWO

The Candidate

❖
❖

Huey Long opened his law practice in Winnfield with bright prospects. In 1912, Julius, the district attorney for Winn and Jackson parishes, turned over much of his civil practice to Huey and made him a partner. The partnership broke up less than two months later. Not satisfied by civil practice, Huey wanted to defend accused criminals whom Julius was prosecuting. The real conflict, however, was personal. Julius considered himself the senior partner and expected Huey's gratitude for providing him clients. Huey could neither take orders nor accept his status as junior partner; he considered himself superior to Julius and did not hesitate to tell him. Reading one of Julius's briefs, Huey remarked that it "wasn't worth a damn" and tore it up. Julius promptly dissolved the partnership.

Huey paid a painter 50 cents to make a sign reading "Huey P. Long, Lawyer," and opened his own practice. He rented a windowless 8'-x-10' office above the Bank of Winnfield from his Uncle George for $4 a month, furnishing it with a pine table, three law books, a kerosene lamp, and two kitchen chairs. Unable to afford a telephone, he arranged for the proprietor of an adjoining shoe store to take calls.

At first no clients came, so Huey took part-time jobs. He became the Winnfield correspondent for Shreveport's three dailies, the *Times*, the *Journal*, and the *Caucasian*. Long wrote up accounts of political meetings he attended, publicizing his activities and minimizing mention of his political enemies. After less than a year all three papers fired him because he refused to file a story about a two-parish rally for Louisiana's commissioner of agriculture. Long explained that the meeting was not news; only a few people had attended. He said he resented giving free publicity to insignificant politicians.

Huey's other job was more lucrative. He became a traveling salesman for the Never Fail Company of Greenfield, Ohio, selling suspenders, garters, and oil cans with built-in pumps. Because electric lights were rare in north Louisiana, Huey earned most of his commissions from the cans, which brought him more money than his law practice. He thought he could cover more territory in a car, so in 1915 he borrowed 50 percent of the purchase price of a second-hand Model T Ford from his employer, J. A. Harps. Although he bought the car for his selling, he knew it might also be useful for political campaigning. Long had already boasted to Harps that he planned to run for office and was anxious to travel his region and meet people who might be useful to him politically. "Away from this place I have a certain reputation," he explained, "as I have made many flashy appearances that will be of great benefit to me in the politics of this state so soon as I achieve the proper success at the place where I am located as an actual lawyer as well as get a little more age and knowledge and live comfortably at the same time." Long predicted that he would soon put all his competitors out of business, as he had done selling Faultless Starch. Harps made the loan but was unimpressed with Huey's boasts. He considered Long arrogant and unreliable, and when he did not repay the loan Harps fired him and repossessed the car.

Huey dabbled in politics. In 1915 he flattered John H. Overton, a wealthy Alexandria politician, by urging him to run for governor. He also suggested to several men, including state Supreme Court Justice Charles A. O'Neil, that they run against U.S. Senator Joseph E. Ransdell. He also sought the support of Ransdell, and of Senator Robert F. Broussard, for appointment as assistant United States attorney for his district. Ransdell was unaware of Long's duplicity, although he and Broussard decided to support another candidate for the position. Huey was bitterly disappointed.

Long's law practice grew. In one case he defended a cousin accused of stealing a pig; Huey convinced the jury that his cousin was the victim of a vicious smear and he received the pig as his fee. Long obtained extensive publicity from handling a suit by a poor widow, Martha E. DeLoach, against his Uncle George's bank. Neither Long nor DeLoach could afford the $100 necessary to post bond for the trial, so Huey borrowed the money from S. J. Harper, one of the directors of the bank and a state senator, a wealthy eccentric devoted to the underdog. He had known the Long family for many years and favored economic leveling. He was also an anti-Semite who believed Jewish bankers incited wars, and endorsed the authenticity of a notorious anti-Jewish forgery, *The Protocols of the Elders of Zion*. Long also believed in plots by bankers. In the DeLoach case Huey aroused sympathy for a client no other attorney would accept. He arranged for the indigent woman's children, clad in rags, to sit directly in front of the jury box. Persuading the jurors that the woman was the victim of a heartless institution, Long won the case.

Much of Long's legal business came from workers injured on the job, who sought compensation from their employers. Huey handled more compensation cases than any other Winnfield attorney, causing some lawyers to dismiss him as an ambulance chaser. He received as much as 50 percent of the award as his fee, yet his profits were hurt by a 1914 law that limited compensation to a maximum of $300 for job-related injuries. Long drafted several amendments and persuaded Harper to introduce them in the legislature, then accompanied him to Baton Rouge to testify before a Senate committee. This was the first time Long had seen the legislature in session and he was not impressed. When he tried to speak, Huey was silenced and the senators reported all his amendments unfavorably. Harper was more successful on the floor, however, and some of Long's amendments were enacted.

When the United States entered World War I, Long's legal practice was one of the larger ones in Winnfield, and he had no desire to serve in the armed forces. "I wasn't mad at anybody over there," he said. A daughter, named Rose, had been born to the Longs in April 1917, and Huey sought a deferment on the grounds that he was the sole support of his wife, child, and aged father. His siblings, who were contributing to Hugh's support, resented Huey's claim that he was carrying the burden. Earl, who was earning good money as a salesman and hoped to avoid conscription, also claimed Hugh as a dependent. Huey also filed for exemption as a public official—a notary public. None of the Longs served.

Long's friend, Harper, was against the war. The old battler announced that he would run for the U.S. House of Representatives against incumbent James B. Aswell on an antiwar platform. Harper denounced conscription in a campaign pamphlet entitled "The Issues of the Day: Financial Slavery, Free Speech." If the nation insisted on drafting young men it should compel the wealthy to pay for it by seizing large fortunes. Sympathetic to Harper's plea for the confiscation of wealth, Long wrote a letter to the New Orleans *Item* summarizing an article in the *Saturday Evening Post*, with statistics gleaned from a report issued by President Wilson's Industrial Relations Commission. Between 1899 and 1910, Long argued, "the wealth of the nation trebled, yet the masses owned less in 1910 than in 1890. . . . Wealth is fast accumulating in the hands of the few." He added a religious argument, "There is not the opportunity for Christian uplift and education and cannot be until there is economic reform." Long continued to use the same statistics all his life, and the letter became the basis of his proposals to redistribute wealth, culminating in his Share Our Wealth Society.

During the wartime hysteria, Harper was charged with violating the Espionage Act by obstructing the draft. He hired Huey and Julius to defend him. Although Huey later claimed credit for Harper's acquittal, Julius, as senior counsel, developed the strategy. Julius restrained his hot-headed younger brother from alienating the judge and jury by kicking him under the defense table. Despite the acquittal, Harper's political career was destroyed and he resigned from the legislature.

Long made his debut as a political candidate in 1918. In 1915 he had confided to Harley Bozeman that he planned to run against Julius for district attorney in 1916. Bozeman, realizing that Huey's candidacy would hurt both brothers, suggested that Huey wait and run for a higher office, on the Louisiana Railroad Commission. It was the only state office with no age qualification. The commission was potentially powerful in the hands of an imaginative politician. Established by the Louisiana Constitution of 1898 to regulate railroads, telegraphs, telephones, steamboats, and other means of transportation and communication, its three members, elected for staggered six-year terms, were paid $3,000 a year plus expenses. The position would ensure financial security and provide the opportunity to become known statewide. Commissioners were elected by district: one from the New Orleans area, one from south Louisiana, and one from north Louisiana. The north Louisiana district in which Long resided was the largest geographically, with 28 of the state's 64 parishes. Largely rural, it was ideal for Huey's brand of oratory; it included the area he had worked as a traveling salesman.

His campaign was carefully planned and amply financed, and Huey outworked his older opponents because he wanted the position so badly. It was unusual for a candidate to devote such assiduous attention to details. Most campaigns were conducted by word of mouth with a few speeches and a handful of newspaper advertisements. Long hit the backwoods constituents like a lumberjack clear-cutting a forest, harvesting voters one at a time and leaving none untouched. In 1916, two years before the election, he began corresponding with police jurors, school board members, justices of the peace, and constables in his district. He also corresponded with their defeated opponents, who might be receptive to change.

The incumbent, Burk A. Bridges, of Homer, in Claiborne Parish, was a man of moderate wealth who, like Huey, had been a traveling salesman. Elected in 1912, he expected little difficulty in being reelected, failed to recognize that his job was in jeopardy, and conducted a quiet, personal campaign; a few newspaper advertisements emphasized his experience and described him as a "high class gentleman, moral and courageous." Three other candidates entered the race, which helped

Long. One of his supporters, Winn Parish Tax Assessor O. K. Allen, consummated an alliance with a rival candidate; if the rival or Long failed to make the second primary, the loser would support the winner. Similar offers were made to other candidates.

The whole Long family campaigned. Julius, Huey's campaign manager, helped to write newspaper copy and circulars, and delivered speeches. Earl paid Huey's filing fee and contributed money. Long established his headquarters at the home of his wife's parents in Shreveport, where Rose stuffed envelopes and made telephone calls. Huey, Bozeman, and Earl toured rural areas that other politicians considered insignificant. Huey promised lower utility rates and increased services, labeling the railroad companies "tools of Wall Street."

Bridges led the first Democratic primary in 1918 with a plurality of 2,000 votes, but had to face Long, who finished second, in a runoff. Huey got the endorsements of the three defeated candidates and attacked Bridges, accusing him of collusion with the railroad companies to fix rates. The special interests, he claimed, supported the incumbent because "it is but natural for the railroads to support the man who will allow them the highest rate of profit." Long gained additional backing from Mayor John H. Overton of Alexandria, who ran for the U.S. Senate in the first primary. Although Overton lost the runoff, he carried 17 of the 28 parishes in Long's district and his support lent credibility to the Long campaign. Huey received funds from Allen, a gentle, amiable man, the only elected parish official in the district who had endorsed Long before the second primary. A self-made businessman of moderate wealth, he came from a family much poorer than Long's. Although older than Long, he allowed Huey to dominate him. Just a few weeks after his twenty-fifth birthday, Huey defeated Bridges by 635 votes in the runoff. He carried only 4 of the 28 parish seats, but amassed huge majorities in the rural areas; generally, the larger the town, the more poorly Long fared. The race attracted little statewide attention, and Long polled only 7,286 votes. Not a single parish in the district produced a turnout as high as 50 percent.

Shortly after the election Long moved his family to Shreveport, Louisiana's second largest city. The booming oil city was lucrative for attorneys, and Huey also wished to enhance his political contacts and his accessibility. Huey invited Julius to join him in a partnership and the older brother accepted, but their relationship quickly deteriorated. Neither could accept the status of junior partner and within two months they had dissolved the partnership. Huey and Julius bickered for the rest of their lives.

After Julius's departure Huey built a profitable practice that involved only a few major cases. In 1921 Long invited another young Shreveport attorney, Cecil Morgan, to become his partner. Morgan, who needed business, declined because he considered Huey an unethical attorney. (Years later, after Long's election as governor and Morgan's election to the state House of Representatives, Morgan led the movement to impeach Huey.)

Although Long was more concerned with building a political career than acquiring wealth, he had no aversion to money. His income tax returns for 1921, a typical year, indicate that he earned $13,450, $3,000 of which was his salary as a railroad commissioner. Huey soon recognized that oil represented a more promising avenue to wealth than politics or law. He accepted some oil properties and stocks as legal fees and participated in the creation of at least three small oil companies. In 1917 oil was struck at Pine Island, near Shreveport, and properties there became valuable. When the United States entered World War I and demand for petroleum soared, Huey's $1,050 interest in Pine Island appreciated. The Standard Oil Company offered him $8,500 for his stock, but Long demanded $12,000. Then, as quickly as the boom had materialized, it collapsed at the end of the war. After the Navy cancelled contracts calling for future oil purchases, Standard reduced its oil purchases from Pine Island and cut its price. Long charged Standard, whose pipelines were the only transportation available for north Louisiana oil, with attempting to drive small producers out of business. Standard replied that it was only responding to the market and offered to transport Pine Island crude free of charge if the producers could find buyers. They could not. "I had gone to sleep one night with transactions all ready to be closed for options and equities I had acquired which meant that I might some day be mentioned among the millionaires," Long wrote, "to awake in the morning to read that nothing I had was of value because the three pipeline companies said so." Having failed to become a millionaire, Long developed an intense antipathy toward those who did.

Unfortunately for Standard, Huey Long was a commissioner on the governmental body that regulated pipelines. Eager to exercise his newly acquired political clout, he proposed that railroad commissioners wear gold badges "so that people will know us, and give us the respect we're due." The state had two weapons the oil industry feared: the power to tax and the authority to regulate rates charged by common carriers. Long drafted legislation to regulate Standard. He proposed a stiff severance tax on the oil industry and a bill making Standard's pipelines subject to rate regulation by his commission.

Long discovered that by attacking the corporation he won popular support. Outside of Baton Rouge, where its refinery dominated the local economy, the company was resented, particularly by independent oilmen. In 1920 Long demanded that Governor Ruffin G. Pleasant summon a special session of the legislature to deal with severance taxes and pipeline regulation. After Pleasant refused, Long made the oil question an issue in the 1920 gubernatorial campaign. The chief candidates were Frank P. Stubbs, a World War I hero, and John M. Parker, a wealthy cotton broker who owned a home in New Orleans and a plantation in St. Francisville. Parker was a quintessential southern progressive, a politician of national stature, and one of the few intimates of both Theodore Roosevelt and Woodrow Wilson.

Parker loathed the New Orleans machine and devoted much of his career to fighting it. He believed it rigged elections and bought votes and he organized the Good Government League to combat it. Parker ran for governor unsuccessfully as a Progressive in 1916. Later that year he was nominated as the vice-presidential nominee of the Progressive Party, but the ticket withdrew after Roosevelt declined the presidential nomination. Subsequently he worked as Louisiana Food Administrator during World War I, part of a national operation directed by Herbert Hoover.

Parker, running in 1920 as a Democrat, knew that he needed to improve his 1916 vote total in north Louisiana. He agreed to support measures to regulate the oil industry and Long, in return, pledged to campaign for him in the north. The two had antithetical personalities: Parker was restrained, led by example, and radiated integrity; Long was uninhibited, led by prodding, and emphasized results. Parker delivered short, flat, factual speeches; Long orated. Each was stubborn and opinionated, and although they might collaborate, only one could lead.

Long realized Parker was likely to win, and he knew that by campaigning for Parker he could make himself better known. Parker, in fact, carried north Louisiana by a scant 761 votes and won by about 12,000 votes statewide in the January election. Long claimed credit for the victory and tried to set the agenda for the administration. Parker neither considered Long his most valuable ally nor would he accept Long's recommendations. He compromised on the pipeline and tax bills and invited Standard attorneys to participate in writing them. The outcome satisfied most independent oilmen, but not Long, who charged that Standard ran the state and that Parker had traded in "offices which belong to the people and bartered them away in a manner unbecoming an ancient ruler of a Turkish domain." He distributed such intemperate circulars that a motion to impeach him passed in the House. Although Long was never tried, Representative John Dymond moved "to appoint a lunacy commission to inquire into the sanity of Huey P. Long."

When Long continued to pen angry circulars, Parker sued him for libel. Long's defense team, headed by Julius, included James Palmer and Robert E. Reed. (Long subsequently named his younger son Palmer Reed Long.) Both sides claimed victory at the trial in Baton Rouge. Long was convicted on two counts, but the sentence was only 30 days, suspended, on one count, and a fine of $1 on the other.

Although Long had opposed Parker's call for a convention to draft a new state constitution in 1921, the new document strengthened his hand. The Railroad Commission was transformed into the more powerful Public Service Commission with the incumbents retaining their seats. In November, 1921, Commissioner John T. Michel, a Long opponent, died. His successor, Francis Williams, a New Orleanian, like Huey, opposed the Old Regulars. When Williams assumed his seat in April, 1922, he and Long elected Huey chair. With Long as chair, the commission became supercharged, reversing decisions to permit utility rate increases and denying new ones. Long depicted himself as the champion of consumers exploited by greedy corporations. The most dramatic case concerned the Cumberland Telephone and Telegraph Company, which served north Louisiana. In 1920 Shelby Taylor and Michel had voted, over Long's objections, to permit the company to raise its rates by 20 percent. After Williams succeeded Michel, he and Long decided to reconsider the increase and ultimately voted to reduce it by 50 percent. Moreover, they ordered the company to refund to its customers the difference between the old rate and the newly reduced rate, a total of about $440,000. It would have been cheaper to give consumers credits on bills than to require refund checks, but the latter was far more dramatic. Every customer who received a check in the mail was grateful to Long. When he ran for governor in 1923 Long reprinted and distributed thousands of copies of his order compelling Cumberland to pay the refund.

Although Long's rhetoric was harshly anticorporation, he was more conciliatory in private. His political opponents, including Julius, claim that he permitted selective rate increases in return for bribes and political support; for example, Long compelled the Southwestern Gas and Electric Company to reduce its charges for electricity but simultaneously, and quietly, permitted the company to raise rates for natural gas. In return, Southwestern donated $10,000 to Long's gubernatorial campaign in 1923. Some corporations that Long publicly chastised he privately courted, and Long's friends included railroad and utility magnates. Even Cumberland was compensated for its compulsory refund. Long permitted an increase in charges to customers that netted Cumberland $500,000 in a single year.

Because Long had boasted of his ambition to become governor since boyhood, it came as no surprise when he announced his candidacy for the January, 1924, Democratic gubernatorial primary on the day he reached the minimum age of 30. He had a narrow window of opportunity. The previous day he would have been too young; two days later the qualification period expired. Palmer, who helped to defend Huey in the libel suit, had already qualified, and in 1921 Long had promised to support him. When Huey announced his candidacy Palmer felt betrayed and withdrew because he had no chance of winning.

Long's chief opponents were Hewitt Bouanchaud, the incumbent lieutenant governor, and Henry L. Fuqua, warden of the state penitentiary. Both were older and more experienced than Long, and had larger campaign treasuries and greater organizational and journalistic support. However, neither could match Long's rhetoric. Long in 1923 appeared a crusading idealist. He was not as effective a speaker as he later became, but already he could stir crowds like no other Louisiana politician.

Most politicians bet on the more prominent candidates and few expected Long to reach the second primary. Bouanchaud, a French Catholic from the town of New Roads, was Parker's choice. He obtained the support of the New Orleans New Regulars, a dissident Choctaw faction led by Colonel John P. Sullivan, and was certain to win Catholic south Louisiana. Fuqua, although a southern Louisianan, was a Protestant. He had southern support as a local son and would compete with Long for the Protestant vote in northern Louisiana. Furthermore, because the Old Regulars endorsed him, he had the strongest organization in the New Orleans.

Long's desire to unite the rural voters of north and south Louisiana foundered upon the issue of the Ku Klux Klan. A resurrected version of the Reconstruction Klan founded in Georgia in 1915, it appeared in Louisiana in 1920. Louisiana was a fertile field for organizers because there was animosity among white Protestants against both blacks and Catholics. The first klaverns were organized in New Orleans but Shreveport soon became the state headquarters of the Klan.

Louisiana klansmen wanted to dismiss Catholic teachers from the public schools, abolish parochial schools, and suppress illegal liquor but were not notably successful. At its peak in 1922 the Louisiana Klan boasted 25,000 members, and 2,500 affiliated women. Governor Parker, although both his father and grandfather had been members of the original Klan, opposed the masked order. One reason he supported Bouanchaud was because his lieutenant governor was as firmly anti-Klan as he was.

Bouanchaud made opposition to the Klan his major campaign issue. He announced that he wanted no Klan votes and would appoint no klansman to his administration. Fuqua was equivocal but he, like Bouanchaud, pledged to outlaw the wearing of masks and require secret organizations to file membership lists.

Long, a native of the region where the Klan was strongest, solicited support from Louisiana klaverns. The leader of the Monroe Klan endorsed Long and cousin Swords Lee made Long an honorary member. Long said he preferred to talk about "the Invisible Empire of the Standard Oil Corporation."

The Klan issue was thrust into the 1923 gubernatorial campaign by a macabre episode in Morehouse Parish, a center of local Klan activity, a north-central parish in the heartland of the Klan. The tiny agricultural community of Mer Rouge developed an economic and social rivalry with the larger, younger lumber community of Bastrop. Two Bastrop men, F. Watt Daniel and Thomas F. Richards, incurred the enmity of parish Klan leaders and ridiculed the Klan. Klansmen kidnapped Richards from the garage where he worked and beat him. Unfortunately for him, he recognized several of his abductors.

On August 25 robed klansmen seized five men leaving a parish barbecue. Three were released, but Daniel and Richards were never again seen alive. A massive search was fruitless. A grand jury empaneled to investigate reported on September 8 that it was unable to identify the kidnappers or determine the fate of the victims. Nine of the 12 jurors and the district attorney were klansmen.

Parker requested federal help to find the missing men. Evidence that Arkansas klansmen were involved provided grounds for federal participation. President Warren G. Harding, however, was not sympathetic; in fact he was a klansman himself.

Since neither the federal government nor the parish would act, the responsibility was Parker's. In December he ordered the National Guard to assist in the search. The men were found in Lake Lafourche. On the evening of December 22, klansmen, who tied weights to the bodies to sink them, attempted to bury them under tons of mud by exploding dynamite in the vicinity. The explosion had just the opposite effect; it freed the weights and the bodies floated to the surface.

Pathologists concluded the men had been mutilated before death. Their hands and feet had been severed, their arms and legs broken, their heads and chests crushed, and they had been castrated. Journalists rushed to Louisiana. Parker held open hearings in Morehouse and another parish grand jury was assembled, yet returned no indictments. The state indicted 18 klansmen for carrying illegal weapons and four of them were convicted and fined $10 each. The murders were unsolved.

The timing of the incident and the widespread attention it received made the Klan an issue of great magnitude in 1923. It created an obstacle to Long's ambition to transcend Louisiana's regional differences. Although most south Louisiana Catholics resented the Klan, north Louisiana Protestants supported it, denouncing the publicity as a papal plot. Under any circumstances Long's task would have been formidable; the Mer Rouge murders made it impossible.

Moreover, the state's political establishment preferred Fuqua or Bouanchaud. Bouanchaud had the patronage controlled by the Parker administration. Fuqua's backers included former governors Pleasant and J. Y. Sanders, perhaps Louisiana's most influential politician. Sanders had been governor from 1908 to 1912 and U.S. Representative from 1917 to 1921. He and his son, J. Y., Jr., also a prominent politician, detested Long.

Long was weak in New Orleans, where only the Independent Regulars, a small splinter group that Williams and his brother Gus led, supported him. Huey had less newspaper support than Bouanchaud or Fuqua and less money. Nonetheless, he had the money to stage a creditable campaign. A few corporations gave Long money in exchange for favors he granted as a commissioner. Huey's family and Winnfield friends, such as Bozeman and Allen, contributed generously. His distant cousin Swords Lee, who expected to receive state construction contracts, gave $10,000. William K. Henderson, a Shreveport businessman, gave $10,000 and time on his radio station.

Long broadcasted a few radio speeches but there were only 8,000 radio sets in Louisiana in 1923. More important was his use of trucks with amplifiers attached. Long campaigned in remote areas the other candidates skipped. In rural Louisiana humble people—farmers, repairmen, and small merchants—introduced him. Speaking the idiom of rural people and understanding their problems, he was best among farmers and their families, puncturing the pomposity of city slickers and lambasting the corporations. Sometimes he gave $25 or $50 to ministers of small, fundamentalist churches and asked them to urge their congregants to consider him. He later remarked that the gifts represented the best money he ever spent.

Long promised to construct a modern highway system and to provide free textbooks to schoolchildren. He also pledged to build toll-free bridges, to make the state penitentiary self-supporting, to place union representatives on state boards, and to increase workers' compensation benefits. He told rural audiences he would abolish the state Conservation Commission, and permit unlimited hunting and fishing year-round. Borrowing an idea from the Populists, he suggested the construction of statewide warehouses where farmers could store crops, receiving negotiable notes with the crops as collateral. He promised to pipe natural gas for heating to New Orleans and to pave Claiborne Avenue, one of the city's main streets. All this would be done without raising taxes.

Long condemned the Parker administration for excessive spending, particularly for a new campus for Louisiana State

University. "Our kind don't need college," he told rural people. "Show me a man who has ever gone to an agricultural college and then gone home and made a living off a farm, and I'll put him in Ringling Brothers' Circus." Parker's new buildings were "an act of Executive vanity." Long used wit, ridicule, and invective. His few written speeches were pretentious and verbose.

The campaign of 1923 was notable for its decibel level. Long termed his rivals "the Gold Dust Twins," creations of Parker. He claimed Confederate veterans lacked pensions and patients were freezing in state hospitals; he complained that the Highway Commission was graft-ridden.

Huey magnified kernels of truth into hyperbolic ridicule. His opponents were too dignified to reply, but some of their supporters were not. They charged that Huey was a physical coward, a slacker during World War I, and a heavy drinker. A Standard Oil official said Long's speeches were of "as much moment as the braying of an ass or the yelping of a locoed coyote." Former Governor Pleasant denounced Huey as a "vainglorious, egotistical and selfish . . . pompous, inflated, chesty, loose-mouthed rattletrap" who uttered a "venomous volume of vulgar invectives." The staid New Orleans *Times-Picayune* observed shortly before the election that "Huey P. Long, by his irresponsible and violent utterances, his proved perversions of recorded fact, his vicious tirades against decent men upon whom the commonwealth has honored, and his silly denunciations of the Greater University and Agricultural College, has proved himself unfit for the post of governor."

On January 15, Bouanchaud received 84,162 votes (35 percent) to 81,382 for Fuqua (34 percent) and 73,985 (31 percent) for Long. Observers were astounded by the large vote for Long. He carried all north Louisiana parishes but 3, with majorities in 21 and pluralities in 7. Only Huey's paltry 12,000 votes in New Orleans denied him a place in the runoff. Long knew what to do to win the next election: He must poll a larger vote in New Orleans, or he must carry the rural parishes in the south as well as in the north. The latter was more feasible.

Long liked to boast that his defeat had been a fluke; heavy

rains throughout the state prevented a heavy turnout. "I have only the rains to blame for not being the next governor," he complained. Although bad weather made some roads in north Louisiana impassable, it also rained in south Louisiana and in New Orleans, and in the city, although the roads were better, the number of voters who remained home was great.

Both remaining candidates sought Long's endorsement, but he refused. Had he been less proud, an endorsement of Fuqua would have been politically expedient, because everyone knew that few of Long's Protestant supporters in north Louisiana would vote for the Catholic Bouanchaud. However, Huey had labeled his opponents surrogates of Parker and remained hostile toward them. He also wanted to be free to criticize the victor of the second primary. Bouanchaud could win only if he could carry New Orleans, because he was certain to lose in the north. However, his task was hopeless. He had trailed Fuqua in the Crescent City in the first primary and the Old Regular machine was firmly committed to Fuqua. During the runoff Bouanchaud attempted to enhance his appeal to the poor by adopting Long's pledge to provide free textbooks. In the February 19 election, Fuqua polled 125,880 votes to 92,006 for Bouanchaud, carrying New Orleans by 14,540 votes and the country parishes by 19,334 votes.

Throughout the campaign Rose remained in Shreveport with the children. Huey was accompanied by an attractive brunette, Alice Lee Grosjean, 18, whom he hired as his private secretary. Intelligent and discreet, she became the custodian of Long's campaign funds while away from headquarters. Alice had quit high school at 15 to marry James Terrell, a young Arkansan, but soon they separated. When she met Huey she was living alone, working as a secretary, yet she did not divorce her husband until 1928. Grosjean became Huey's mistress.

Long was uncomfortable in the presence of women and never treated any woman as his equal. His crude manners and domineering personality alienated most women, even though some were intrigued by his power. Grosjean and Long remained intimate until his death; Rose resented this, although not enough to leave him.

Huey realized he must advance incrementally toward the governor's mansion. In September, 1924, he ran for reelection to the Public Service Commission. In the same primary voters would elect a U.S. Senator. By winning impressively and supporting successful candidates he could add to his prestige and build alliances. Long faced two challengers to his seat, State Senator Walter L. Bagwell and William C. Barnette, an attorney who had represented the Klan in the Mer Rouge incident. Barnette concluded that he had no chance to win and withdrew, but Bagwell staged a strenuous, if ineffective, campaign, running on a probusiness platform that provided Long ammunition to discredit him. Bagwell claimed that Huey "abused and humiliated" attorneys for corporations at meetings, complaining that "heads of corporate interests have been treated at times as though they were criminals before a police court in the downtown district, and in many instances they have been refused common courtesies by the chairman." Long overwhelmed Bagwell, winning 45,000 votes to only 8,600 for his rival, polling a majority in every parish in the district, totaling 83.9 percent.

In the Senate primary incumbent Joseph E. Ransdell ran for reelection against Huey's archenemy, Shreveport Mayor Lee Emmett Thomas. Long initially was neutral because both candidates had supported Fuqua. However, a week before the election he intervened and staged a speaking tour for Ransdell. Ransdell, although a north Louisianan, was a Catholic and Long's support for him generated sympathy among Catholic voters. Furthermore, Thomas's backers were anti-Long; thus Huey would not lose any friends.

The alliance was nevertheless uneasy and neither party was comfortable. Long's chief contribution was to rebut Thomas's charges that Ransdell sympathized with the doctrine of social equality for blacks. The evidence for this was that Ransdell had addressed a letter to a black Republican about patronage using the generic salutation "mister." Long defended Ransdell as a white supremacist and claimed that it was Thomas, not the senator, who fraternized with blacks; Thomas must have received a copy of the letter from the black man. "For the first time in many years, Mr. Thomas furnishes us with the example of a native white Louisianan who would like to go to the United States Senate on help furnished by a negro Republican," he charged. Then he added sexual imagery to appeal to puritanical north Louisiana, saying of Thomas: "I was against him before he took Cohen [the black man] to his bosom and snuggled with him on a political bed on a mattress made and manufactured by distributors of yellow falsehoods." (Ironically, when Long ran against Ransdell in 1930 he used the Cohen letter to charge that Ransdell indeed did believe in social equality.) Ransdell easily defeated Thomas by 20,000 votes and even the hostile *Times-Picayune* gave credit to Long: "Politicians, whether enamored with Huey Long or not," it stated, "give him credit for breaking into the Thomas strongholds in north Louisiana."

By supporting Ransdell, Long solidified north Louisiana, attracted Catholic backers, and neutralized a potential adversary. Another opportunity appeared in the primary contest for U.S. Senator in September 1926. The incumbent, Edwin S. Broussard, opposed prohibition and favored tariff protection for sugar planters, unpopular positions in north Louisiana. Still, Long and Broussard needed one another because each was strong where the other was weak. If Long could sell Broussard in Protestant northern Louisiana, he might win the support of Broussard's Cajun followers in the south. Moreover, Huey could not support J. Y. Sanders, whom he hated.

Long spoke for Broussard throughout the state, where he was introduced as the "next governor of Louisiana." Broussard did not pledge to support Huey in the next election, but Long knew the senator's gratitude would be an asset. Huey praised Broussard's advocacy of free bridges and denounced Sanders for serving interests that wanted to build a toll bridge at the northern approach to New Orleans over Lake Pontchartrain. The *Times-Picayune,* which had denounced Huey in 1924, praised his efforts for Broussard. Long helped to limit Sanders's majority in north Louisiana, enabled Broussard to eke out a 3,500-vote victory, and received publicity in the Cajun south. Once rural southern Louisianans became Longites not even Broussard could change them.

Long's position on the commission had grown tenuous because of his political activities after 1924. He had also broken with Williams, whose mayoral aspirations he refused to support. Long vindictively denied Williams funds for travel and expenses to conduct official business, fired his friends, and allied himself with the third member, his old foe, Shelby Taylor, whose seat was at stake in 1926.

Taylor's opponent was popular State Representative Dudley J. LeBlanc, who called himself "the Huey P. Long of southwest Louisiana," a colorful Cajun with a regional following who enjoyed a fabulous business career. He invented an alcoholic patent medicine called Hadocol, and promoted it so successfully that in the early 1950s it outsold Bayer aspirin. The Cajun became a millionaire before the Food and Drug Administration took Hadocol off the market. LeBlanc, an effective speaker and storyteller, had supported Long and Huey encouraged him to enter the race. Long's break with Williams posed a problem, because Williams and LeBlanc were allies. If the two joined forces on the commission, they could outvote Long. Therefore, Long asked LeBlanc to withdraw, a suggestion that LeBlanc angrily dismissed. Huey then campaigned for Taylor, but LeBlanc won easily.

At the first commission meeting he attended, LeBlanc voted with Williams to replace Long as chair with Williams. From then on, Long rarely attended meetings. He gave up his effort to have Standard Oil declared a public utility subject to commission regulation, and did not exercise his right to examine some of the company's books. Occasionally he provided technical assistance to the commission, and in return received fees.

Long devoted more time to his law practice and built a profitable business in southern Arkansas. He represented a man who sued the Commercial National Bank of Shreveport, winning a settlement that netted a fee of $50,000. He built a $40,000 home in an exclusive Shreveport neighborhood. His ambition for the governorship never flickered.

CHAPTER THREE

Campaigns for Governor

❖
❖

After his 1923 campaign almost everyone expected Huey Long to run again in the gubernatorial primary of January 1928. The Klan had largely disintegrated in Louisiana by 1928 after Governor Fuqua redeemed his pledge to dismantle it. In May, 1924, he introduced three anti-Klan bills in the legislature. One prohibited the wearing of masks except during Mardi Gras; a second defined assault by a masked person as a felony; another required all secret organizations to file membership lists with the secretary of state, with the proviso that individuals who resigned before the law took effect would not be listed.

This grace period gained Fuqua the Klan's support for the bills. Most members of the legislature who were klansmen voted for all three bills to avoid severe restrictions. The cooperation of Louisiana klansmen incensed the national leaders, and Imperial Wizard Hiram Wesley Evans fired the Bayou State's chieftans, replacing them with a triumvirate that included Swords Lee. Fuqua's laws accomplished their purpose. Before registration became effective on September 1, the Louisiana Klan dissolved. State klansmen who claimed membership only in the national organization did not have to register. The Louisiana Klan would never again be a major factor in politics.

The Klan also declined nationally. The role of fraternal orders in American life diminished and vigilante justice was not respectable. Fear of Bolshevism receded, as did hostility toward immigrants, whose numbers fell after the Immigration Act of 1924.

Local developments favored Long. Martin Behrman, the boss of the Old Regulars, died in 1925. His successor, Arthur J. O'Keefe, lacked Behrman's experience, influence, and stamina. Equally important, Fuqua died on October 11, 1926, two years before his term expired. Thus, before the 1927 campaign, two of the more formidable anti-Long state politicians were dead.

Before Fuqua's death, Lieutenant Governor Oramel H. Simpson had planned to run for governor; he used patronage during his short tenure to create support. Previous Louisiana governors had manipulated patronage, but Simpson was more blatant because he had just two years to build a following. Simpson also adopted some of the popular planks from Long's 1923 platform: free bridges, textbooks, highways, and improved hospitals. The Highway Commission added thousands of employees. Simpson pledged to suppress gambling, appoint women to office, and provide pensions for Confederate veterans and their survivors.

Simpson, clerk of the state House of Representatives for 20 years, did not impress people as a strong candidate. A defector from the ranks of the Old Regulars, with ties to the New Orleans elite, he could not command the support of the machine. An ineffective, pompous campaigner, Simpson delivered speeches mechanically. He drank heavily and bet on horse races, something north Louisiana fundamentalists considered sinful. He was not a factional leader and had no popular issue. Many state politicians considered him a competent lieutenant governor, but thought he lacked the ability to be governor. He found it difficult to raise money because potential contributors considered him unelectable.

The Old Regulars, hostile to Long and believing Simpson inept, tried to recruit a candidate to add rural strength to their New Orleans vote. A political vacuum existed, created by the absence of issues with statewide appeal, except those identified with Long. The weather in the spring of 1927, though, created an issue—a massive natural disaster. The most destructive flood in its history ravaged the Mississippi Valley. Southern

Louisiana, flat and low, was inundated. Secretary of Commerce Herbert Hoover toured the valley and announced that he would propose construction of a flood control system. However, Treasury Secretary Andrew Mellon and President Calvin Coolidge, who hoped to reduce federal spending, wanted the states to contribute to the project, which many Louisianans believed their state could not afford. Into the breach stepped Riley Joe Wilson, U.S. Representative for northeastern Louisiana for 14 years and the ranking minority member on the Flood Control Committee. Wilson had devoted much of his time to flood control. The Old Regulars and Louisiana's political establishment thought he could defeat Long if he emphasized flood control. Like Long, Wilson was a Winn Parish native and a Protestant. If he could stay even with Long in rural north Louisiana, machine support in New Orleans would enable him to win.

Wilson rose from poverty thanks to intelligence and hard work. He had taught school and served as a district judge before becoming a congressman, but because he had been in Congress so long local people had forgotten him. Wilson had not been active in state politics and did not appeal to south Louisianans. Inarticulate and colorless, he was a terrible campaigner. The Regulars realized that he lost votes by delivering dull speeches, so they sent him back to Washington for the final months of the campaign.

Long was the last candidate to announce formally, but he waged the most active campaign. Huey knew he would win north Louisiana and lose urban Louisiana. The swing vote lay in the rural south. Long hoped to carry the section, yet the question remained whether his margin would be sufficient to overcome his expected last-place finish in New Orleans. Turnout was also a factor. Would it be heavier in the city or in the country?

Long entered the race with a better organization than in 1923. He concluded an alliance with John P. Sullivan, leader of the New Regulars, and Sullivan's friend, Colonel Robert Ewing, publisher of daily newspapers in New Orleans, Shreveport, and Monroe. He hoped the Sullivan-Ewing influence would sway New Orleans. By allying himself with Sullivan, however, he damaged his claim to be an idealistic reformer challenging a corrupt machine, for Sullivan had been a lobbyist for liquor interests and was president of the Fair Grounds Race Track. Long's campaign manager, Harvey E. Ellis, resigned to protest Huey's ties to Sullivan.

Ewing's support was more clearly an asset. His newspapers endorsed Long. Huey also received the endorsement of the Hammond daily and about 20 weeklies. The New Orleans *Times-Picayune* backed Simpson and the New Orleans *Item* and the Shreveport *Journal* supported Wilson. The Baton Rouge papers were traditionally neutral in gubernatorial elections. Nevertheless, journalistic endorsements were not a major factor, for many of Long's supporters did not read newspapers and distrusted city publishers.

Long's running mate, Dr. Paul N. Cyr, a feisty French Catholic, added Cajun support and intimidated hecklers at Long rallies. Leander H. Perez, district attorney and political boss of Plaquemines and St. Bernard parishes, also backed Long. The Perez vote was small, but he could deliver it. The sheriffs of St. Bernard and Jefferson parishes backed Long, and some ex-Bouanchaud supporters campaigned for him. Charles L. Pecot, a southern sheriff, succeeded Ellis as Huey's campaign manager. Huey got central Louisiana support from Swords Lee and John H. Overton. Louisiana's U.S. Senators remained benevolently neutral and Long enjoyed the backing of many of their supporters. "It is a mistake to think Huey Long's election in 1928 was solely a revolt of the masses. . . . It was the result of a mass vote plus support of bosses like Sullivan," said Eugene Stanley, who served as Louisiana's attorney general.

Long appealed chiefly to the poor, identifying himself as the voice of the common man. Actually, all three candidates were from humble backgrounds and their platforms were similar. But Long excelled at publicizing himself. He reprinted thousands of copies of his Cumberland refund order and wrote circulars extolling his highway program and his promise to provide free textbooks to children. During his campaign he distributed more than one million simply written and provocative handbills. Huey coined catchy slogans, and used radio and sound trucks. At 34, he was more vigorous and more imaginative than Wilson, 59, and Simpson, 57. All three candidates promised schoolbooks. But Wilson wanted to impose a means test, to give books only to the poor, and Simpson wanted to raise taxes. Long pledged books for everyone without raising taxes.

Huey did not promise to soak the rich in his campaign, but he did convey the impression that he favored the poor. Long assistant Gerald Smith later explained that Huey always phrased promises so that a 6-year-old could understand them. He limited his points to no more than five a speech, so the audience would remember them, and he made bolder and more sweeping promises than his opponents. Smith compared this tactic to promising a child a red bicycle for Christmas. The concept of the state government acting like Santa Claus was new to Louisiana; previously it had acted more like Scrooge.

Long was proud of his ability to outpromise opponents. His son Russell explained that Huey felt one should "promise so blamed much it can't possibly be done so that people will vote for you to see if you can do it. Some things he did very clearly to be elected. And he felt that a promise to be fulfilled got about seven times as many votes as a promise kept." Huey emphasized the tangible benefits rather than how to pay for them. It should have been obvious that he could not produce what he promised without raising taxes. In the 1927 campaign he ran as a fiscal conservative, denouncing deficits and vowing to cut taxes. He proposed to eliminate waste by firing worthless state workers. For example, he condemned the Conservation Commission: "They are hiring men to watch coons on the streets of Shreveport and New Orleans." In a classic outsider's campaign, his principal theme was the vested interests versus the people. There was a degree of truth in this assertion; members of the establishment knew Long threatened their interests, although they did not perceive the magnitude of the threat. Yet if they publicly opposed Long, they played into his hands. In fact, Long had the private backing of wealthy men, special interests, and corporations. He depicted himself as the underdog even though he was not.

Try as they might, Simpson and Wilson could not escape the image that they were part of the establishment that had presided over the ossification of Louisiana. Even their supporters found them uninspiring. Huey mastered crowd psychology; his opponents could have sold their speeches as tranquilizers. If people came to hear Long out of curiosity, farmers stayed home to slop the hogs rather than attend a Simpson rally.

Oratory was important in rural Louisiana, where radios were rare, few people read newspapers, and political rallies were the only entertainment. It did not take much education to impress such audiences. A speaker only had to entertain and persuade them that he cared about their problems. Long, one of them, sold ideas as he had once sold merchandise. His voice was too high-pitched to be pleasant, and he spoke with a slight southern drawl. Unlike many southerners, however, he spoke rapidly, words gushing out in a torrent that overpowered and engulfed rather than mesmerized.

Long had not yet perfected his style. "Huey wasn't a good speaker at first," Congressman Overton Brooks said. "I was disappointed the first time I heard him. His speech lacked coherence, was full of expletives." Huey never observed the traditional formalities of debate. However, he possessed qualities far more important in Louisiana. "He was not what I would call an orator; he was what I would call a showman," one of his lieutenants said. One of his assistants in the 1928 campaign recalled that Long often remarked before a speech, "Watch me vaudeville 'em." Julius wrote: "There is hardly a thing that he will not do to catch or hold a crowd's attention. His opponent usually has some feeling of restraint. It puts him at a disadvantage with Huey." Long was uninhibited on the platform, arms flailing, fingers jabbing. He was never shy. "I can't remember back to a time when my mouth wasn't open whenever there was a chance to make a speech," he said. Long may not have won a debate before the Harvard faculty, but he thrilled the Cajuns along Bayou Lafourche.

Huey could speak convincingly on subjects about which he knew nothing. He was not afraid to bluff. Sometimes he claimed to have "written evidence in my pocket" or a "letter in my hand" to prove a statement. He rejected requests for proof and dismissed charges against him. Huey attacked; he enjoyed mudslinging. Long accused opponents of thievery, sexual perversions, or being part Negro. He lifted ideas and phrases from others and shifted positions shamelessly, sprinkling his speeches with profanity and scripture. "He has been the most profuse user of profanity, vulgarity, foul language, from the day he came of age, who ever lived in the state of Louisiana," Julius wrote. After Huey learned that fundamentalist audiences liked speakers who quoted scripture, he instructed a friend, "Go over to Hirsch and Lehman's store and buy me the best damned Bible they've got."

Long was also indefatigable. When not campaigning, he talked so much that he gargled with antiseptics to soothe a hoarse throat. If he could not dominate a conversation, he walked away. People loved to listen to Huey, but he disliked listening to anyone else. Long could speak for hours without pausing to think or consulting notes. He rarely researched his speeches; he extemporized. One of his key assistants, attorney George Wallace, recalled that Long did not have the patience to read even a newspaper; he merely skimmed the headlines. Consequently, his knowledge of issues was superficial. Although he was effective among the unsophisticated, Long's speeches did not impress the educated, who enjoyed them only as entertainment. When he did write out talks they were clumsy and encumbered with long words. Long's speeches were repetitious, yet people in different localities were unaware that he delivered a standard talk and added local references.

Long excelled at withering invective. Wilson was supported "by the lords, dukes, earls, nabobs, satraps, and rajas," he charged, and also by "plutocrats" and "the self-appointed rulers of money and politics." People chuckled at Long's wild charges even when they did not believe them. He denounced his enemies as "criminals and barflys [sic], little two-bit squirts, promoters of crooked skin games, and yellow dogs." He provoked opponents to reply in kind. Ex-governor Ruffin G. Pleasant called Huey "a coward with the conduct of an egg-sucking yellow dog, and a man who lies with a craven heart like a white-livered popinjay."

Gifted with a quick wit, Long could make an audience laugh at an opponent's expense. Huey invented demeaning nicknames for foes. He was a master storyteller. In 1927 Huey told a joke about Lee Thomas, who was campaigning for Wilson: "Why ladies and gentlemen, a Chinaman, a Fiji Islander and Thomas made a bet as to which one could stay locked up the longest with a pole cat. The Chinaman . . . stayed in ten minutes . . . The Fiji Islander stayed fifteen minutes . . . Thomas went in and stayed five minutes and the pole cat ran out." An enraged Thomas, claiming slander, had Huey arrested, but the judge dismissed the case for the simple reason that the document incorrectly stated the charges.

Long could move audiences to tears, too. At the Evangeline Oak in St. Martinville, where the mythical heroine of a Longfellow poem wept for her lover, Long compared the tribulations of Louisianans with the sorrow of Evangeline: "Give me the chance to dry the eyes of those who still weep here!"

Not all of Long's appeals were emotional. He told voters to address their own interests, pointing out that Wilson had voted against the McNary-Haugen plan to aid farmers and the Fordney-McCumber Tariff to protect sugar and rice from foreign competition. He and Simpson pointed out that if Wilson wanted to provide flood protection, he would be more effective in Congress than as governor.

Long appealed to economic self-interest by promising to provide cheap natural gas for heating in New Orleans rather than expensive synthetic gas. Natural gas had been piped from northern Louisiana to the outskirts of New Orleans, he explained, only to be excluded from the city by special interests. He pledged to pave main thoroughfares in New Orleans, one of the few large cities that still had gravel and dirt roads. The gas and the roads would never materialize if his opponents won, he claimed, because they were puppets of special interests.

Long himself was a special interest politician. He directed his appeals at lower-middle-class rural Louisianans. The polarization Huey provoked was rural versus urban more than it was poor versus rich. The urban poor rarely voted for him because there was little for them in his program. Long shrewdly appealed to rural voters; in 1928, 60 percent of Louisianans lived outside cities. Even small-town people were less enthusiastic about Longism than those in isolated areas.

Huey's promise to construct highways was more attractive to rural than to urban voters. Because roads were largely a parish or city responsibility, the richer parishes, the urban ones, had the better roads. Farmers, on the other hand, found the lack of roads a problem in transporting their produce to market. From the beginning of his career to its conclusion, Long's objective was to win and hold rural Louisiana by a combination of promises, benefits, and oratory that rewarded his followers and neglected or punished those who voted against him.

Huey did not hesitate to fabricate while accusing his opponents of lying. Because his credibility was greater than that of his enemies, rural voters believed Long. His tactics infuriated opponents; during the Long era politics involved violence unusual even in a state notorious for turbulence. Long lived in a hostile environment because once in politics he lived exclusively in cities: New Orleans, Shreveport, and Baton Rouge. He found the lives of the country people he championed unbearably dull.

The campaign of 1927 was hardly dull. On November 15, Long encountered former Governor J. Y. Sanders in the lobby of the Roosevelt Hotel, where Huey had his campaign headquarters. The elderly, overweight Sanders called Huey a liar and Long punched him. Pursued by a man nearly twice his age, Huey fled down the corridor into an elevator, but Sanders squeezed in before the doors shut. As the elevator descended, they resumed their fight. Long emerged with Sanders' torn shirtsleeve and cuff link. He told reporters he had fought "with the abandon of a Bengal tiger" and that it had required four men to pry him off. Sanders' version had Long cringing like "a terror-stricken kitten." The next day the New Orleans *Morning Tribune* featured a map of the hotel with a diagram of Huey's path.

The fracas called attention to an embarrassing facet of

Huey's character: He was a physical coward. Rarely has a politician combined such bellicose oratory with such fear of actual combat. Since childhood no one had ever intimidated Huey intellectually, but others always did his fighting. He surrounded himself with armed bodyguards. "Doubtless there never was a man who reached so high a place in public life and who showed as little physical courage," Julius observed. Long, the confident politician, hated crowds and disliked physical contact with the public. He would not walk around a city block without a companion to protect him. He provoked many fistfights yet never finished them. Sometimes he instructed his bodyguards to beat up reporters and political opponents. His aversion went beyond fighting; he did not like to be touched or even to shake hands. "He had one of the weakest handshakes I've ever seen, real flabby," Judge John T. Hood noted. His enemies, exploiting the southern tradition of manliness, ridiculed Huey's cowardice. They arranged for a one-legged man to hit him. Huey fled.

Physically, Long was not an imposing man. His health declined with age due to insomnia, excessive food and drink, and lack of exercise. By 1927 Long had filled out his 5' 11" frame to about 175 pounds and sported a paunch that expanded over the years. His appearance did not seem very threatening to people who met him; indeed, his pudgy features seemed molded out of putty. His face was full, with puffy jowls, a sagging chin with a pronounced cleft, and a bulbous, upturned nose slightly less exaggerated than a circus clown's. Some thought his face resembled that of baseball slugger Babe Ruth. He had unruly, curly, rust-colored hair, and a light complexion. His brown eyes were large, round, and expressive, shifting from jest to rage in a twinkling.

Long thought he dressed fashionably, but in fact his loud clothes only directed attention to his poor taste. Louisiana voters nevertheless preferred his attire to the drab dress of his old-fashioned opponents. In fact, all three candidates in 1927 were hopelessly provincial. Long wore double-breasted coats and loud ties. Sometimes he wore anachronistic white linen suits and white shoes.

In 1927 Long emphasized youth by strenuous campaigning. The coming years would prove him one of the more effective campaigners in America. Few could equal Long's reservoir of energy. He campaigned with the vigor of a Theodore Roosevelt and the compulsiveness of a Lyndon B. Johnson. Long delivered 600 speeches in 1927. Again, he was willing to address small crowds in remote areas spurned by his opponents.

In rural Louisiana he slept overnight with farm families, paying them a dollar or two, rising early for breakfast, and earning their votes. He pretended more affection for such people than he felt. He enjoyed luxurious hotels and rich food but impressed rural people with his affectation of simple tastes. "You have to convince 'em it's for 'em even if it isn't," he said.

Long was less a commoner than Wilson or Simpson, yet the impression he conveyed was just the opposite. He borrowed metaphors from the kitchen and the barnyard. His crude table manners, chewing of tobacco, and grammatical errors were deliberately cultivated. The people who heard Long speak in 1927 never forgot the experience. He made the masses feel important.

When Long campaigned his adrenaline flowed. He worked while his opponents rested. Huey slept very little, averaging about four hours per night, and even that was fitful. He simply could not relax. Sometimes he worked all day and all night, got drunk, slept it off, then began another marathon. Before going to bed he placed a pencil, tablet, chair, and lamp near his bed so he could jot down inspirations during the night. He expected his aides to be available at all hours. Sometimes he placed dozens of telephone calls after midnight. Longite Judge Isom Guillory remembered, "Often when we were in his hotel room he would talk to us from the bathroom while shaving. Mostly he received us in his pajamas." Every week or 10 days Huey would be overcome by exhaustion and sleep 8 or 10 hours. He required absolute quiet to sleep and refused to use pillows because he believed they disrupted the natural curvature of the body. The manic pace took a toll on Long's health. He was not likely to lead a long, healthy life.

A combination of insomnia, depression, and youthful rebellion drove Long to drink, and by 1927 he had a definite problem. Huey had a low tolerance for alcohol and frequently exceeded it. He often drank alone. His cousin, Otho Long, said that during the 1927 campaign he had to sober Huey up so he could deliver a speech. "He liked dark wine in a tumbler on top of whiskey," Longite Richard Foster recalled. "Or he would drink half a glass of whiskey and a glass of Burgundy." After his election as governor, a Baton Rouge pharmacy delivered a bottle of whiskey daily, and Huey drank himself to sleep. "I've been under the influence more nights of my adult life than I've been sober," he told his bodyguard, Murphy Roden, "and out of this have come some of the most brilliant ideas of my career." Once Huey's friend Jess Nugent told him he could become president if he gave up alcohol and tobacco. "That is too high a price to pay," Long replied.

Abnormal nervousness made Huey sleepless and irascible. He seemed perpetually excited. He did not talk in conversational tones, but shouted, bellowed, or whispered. "He was nervous, curious about everything," Earl remembered. Huey's mind and body were constantly active. "He had the energy of ten men," his friend Harry Gamble said. "It was astounding that anybody born in this semitropical climate could have so much energy." Huey's energy, however, could be a liability. He was too impatient for sustained intellectual activity; his attention span was short and he could not sit at a desk and read for more than a few minutes. For all his brilliance, his inability to concentrate resulted in a superficial knowledge of the world. He possessed sound instincts and an ability to size up friends and foes, and was so quick-witted that he intimidated those who might have objected to his inconsistent ideas.

Huey Long was a man in a hurry. Obsessed by time, he did not indulge in casual conversation. He walked at a trot, eating ravenously or not at all. He could not bear to stand in line or to see anyone served ahead of him. He did not make mild requests; he shouted commands at waiters, cab drivers, and secretaries. He felt he was too important for the trivial details of everyday life; others did them for him. Huey resented time spent sleeping, shaving, or being with his family. Children made him nervous. "I can't live a normal family life," he told Rose.

Huey had no cultural or intellectual interests and no hobbies except golf, which he took up late and played badly. Part of his irascibility and crudeness was due to impatience. "Huey Long was not the sentimental sort," Longite George Wallace said. "He detested subterfuge and finesse, preferring to blast his way through any objections to get the job done without regard for the personal feelings of friends or enemies."

Two accounts by people who knew Huey reveal his desperate race against the clock, his impatience, and his insensitivity. One acquaintance recalled a bird-hunting trip. One of the hunters provided a dog as a pointer, to locate birds on the ground. Huey became impatient and angry because the dog was not pointing right and slit its throat.

The second account involved a drive from New Orleans to Baton Rouge in the governor's limousine with O. K. Allen, Huey's chosen successor as governor, and Long riding in the back seat. Louis Jones, one of Huey's bodyguards, was in front, with the black chauffeur, a man whom Long referred to as "Nigger George." Jones recalled that Huey was sleeping when the car hit a bump that awakened him. Huey ordered George to stop the car and get out. Allen, who rarely objected to Huey's demands, complained, "Don't put my driver out!" Huey snapped, "Shut your goddamn mouth or I will put you out!" Jones took the wheel, and the chauffeur walked back to Baton Rouge.

Such accounts suggest a man who became easily frustrated and could not tolerate the smallest defeat or inconvenience. Although he compromised politically and worked with people he disliked when they could advance his career, he was ruthless and vindictive. He would crucify even a friend for political effect or gain. Paul Flowers, a Longite, commented, "In small groups he could be pretty mean to people around him, that is, his own crowd. Huey liked to break strong people then build them up again once they knew their place." A woman who was a secretary for him said: "He had a temper. I've seen him, when the phone rang once too often, take it up and crash it on the floor, splintering it." Rose said he had a hot temper and alienated some who wanted to be his friends.

Long's career seemed fueled by insecurity. Perhaps he resented his parents, his lack of formal education, and the financial uncertainty of his career as a salesman and in early law practice. He came to believe that results counted, not friendship or humaneness. His inner turmoil created a compulsion that combined a brilliant mind with energy, ruthlessness, and drive.

Although Long lacked the resources and the patience to create a machine organized by ward and precinct, the chaos of Louisiana politics in 1927 made intricate organization unnecessary. He could memorize more than most state politicians could file in writing. His organization consisted of a loose collection of allies emanating from him like the spokes of a wheel. He held meetings and discussed strategy, although he disregarded advice he did not like. Most ideas originated with Huey, and he made the decisions alone, deliberately excluding potential rivals or anyone who might contradict him.

Money fueled the machine. Few men—and no women— were admitted to Long's inner circle unless they had money to contribute. Many had scant sympathy for the masses, and considered Long's identification with the poor a façade. Some had a great deal to lose by redistribution of wealth. They used Huey as cynically as he used them. The perceptive ones who leaped aboard the bandwagon early believed Long would deal them a better hand than anyone else and later they could cash in their chips. They feared and admired Huey and all were awed by his intellect.

Long learned to enjoy material comfort and surrounded himself with luxury; he envied the rich. His chief objective, however, was to win at politics, and money would help. In almost every election in which he ran or sponsored a candidate, Long outspent his opponents. Prudently, he did not publicize his wealth, but cultivated his image as a reformer directing a class revolution.

The men in Long's inner circle, however, were rich yet were

neither highly educated nor aristocratic. Some money came
from his family and friends of relatively modest means. But the
largest contributor was Robert Maestri of New Orleans, who
gave at least $40,000 and became a folk legend in Louisiana
politics. The son of Italian immigrants, Maestri, who inherited
a family furniture business, invested the profits in real estate.
Eventually he owned 500 houses and commercial properties in
New Orleans worth millions. Maestri, though, wanted what he
could not buy: respectability. Like Long, his lack of education
made him insecure. He only completed the third grade. If you
knew him, a New Orleanian said, you would never suspect that
he had a third-grade education; you would suspect that he had
no education. An astute businessman and a perceptive politician, Maestri recognized Long's potential. Other Longites considered him amiable and reliable, if slow-witted and silent.

Perhaps the flashiest of Long's lieutenants was Seymour
Weiss. Like Maestri a southern Louisianan with limited formal
education but substantial native shrewdness, Weiss's rise was
even more meteoric than Maestri's.

Huey was deliberately informal with his finances. He
mingled campaign contributions with his money. His machine
paid most of his personal expenses. He paid in cash, so checks
could not be traced, and Weiss proved a discreet and loyal
treasurer, keeping Long's money in a safe at the Roosevelt
Hotel.

Weiss's business career rivaled Huey's rapid rise in politics.
Born poor, he worked as a hotel clerk in Alexandria, then
moved to New Orleans, where he worked as a shoe salesman,
then as manager of the Roosevelt barber shop. He became,
successively, assistant manager of the hotel, managing director,
vice president, president, and chief owner of the Roosevelt and
a large hotel in New York. By Long's death he was a millionaire
with expensive tastes. Weiss met Huey while Long was resid-
ing in the Roosevelt during the 1927 campaign. Subsequently
he provided Huey with free quarters.

William K. Henderson of Shreveport joined the Long bandwagon and, in 1927, contributed $10,000 plus free radio time.
Like Weiss and Maestri, Henderson was a self-made million-

aire. Henderson was a celebrity when he met Long in Shreveport. He owned the Henderson Iron Works and Supply Company, one of Shreveport's larger enterprises, and operated one of Louisiana's more powerful radio stations. Henderson was one of the first Louisianans to exploit the airwaves as a broadcaster, hosting a nightly program heard throughout the South and the Midwest. He opened each broadcast with, "Hello world, don't go away now," and marketed "Hello World" coffee. A vehement foe of organized labor, Henderson also considered himself the scourge of Wall Street. The popularity of his radio program peaked after the Stock Market Crash of 1929.

Kindred souls, Henderson and Long distrusted concentrated wealth in others. For more than a decade Henderson crusaded against chain stores, which he considered a threat to small business. Long sometimes appeared as a guest on Henderson's show, and also condemned the monopolists. Later, his personal newspapers joined the crusade. Access to Henderson's airwaves helped promote Huey statewide before he became a candidate for governor.

Swords Lee contributed generously to Long's campaign. Other wealthy Longites gave substantial sums, among them Abraham Shushan of New Orleans, John Overton, Leander Perez, and the Fisher family, which operated a south Louisiana shrimping empire. Long developed cozy relationships with independent oil developers, including James A. Noe, William O. Helis, and William C. Feazel. In return for campaign contributions they received lucrative leases on oil deposits on state land, as did Perez and entrepreneur Harvey Peltier of Thibodaux. Railroad and utility magnate Harvey Couch, a faithful contributor to the Long machine, served as an emissary to the business community. Couch provided Long with a private railroad car. Businessmen expecting state contracts if Huey won pitched in, particularly construction companies. Utility companies also contributed, some in return for Long's favors as a public service commissioner, others on the basis of promises of permission to increase charges to consumers and reduced assessments. Even Standard got property tax reductions while Long was governor. Huey solicited contributions from the transportation interests that he regulated as a public service commissioner.

The Long machine never lacked money after 1923. Even businessmen who detested Huey and his policies and considered him a demagogue hedged their bets by contributing. The total was huge and untraceable. Huey insisted on cash donations, and Louisiana law did not require the reporting of contributions.

The Long campaign in 1927 was lavishly financed. Huey paid the poll taxes of potential supporters, printed more circulars, and bought more newspaper and radio advertisements than his rivals. His campaign posters were ubiquitous. Long learned early that name recognition was a key factor in winning elections. He knew intuitively that voters would cast their ballots for a known thief before they would vote for a name they did not recognize. He gained publicity by creating controversies, making outrageous charges, and clowning, partly out of cold calculation, partly because he enjoyed seeing his name in print. He thrived on publicity, good or bad. Journalists found him eminently quotable; audiences found him entertaining. Later, radio networks offered him free time because he generated huge audiences. As entertaining as Will Rogers, he spoke without charge.

Long's charisma, abundant money, and grass roots popularity created an aura of invincibility before the first primary. It was evident from the beginning that he would lead; his opponents fought for the opportunity to oppose him in a runoff. Because Simpson and Wilson competed for a single runoff spot, they directed their attacks more at each other than at Long. Furthermore, antipathy existed between their backers. Simpson was an apostate Old Regular and his backers included two archenemies of the Regulars: the *Times-Picayune* and the Crescent City aristocracy. Long encouraged this animosity. Not only did he supply each candidate with damaging information about the other, he prepared to offer the third-place finisher patronage and money.

As expected, Long led the Democratic first primary on January 17, 1928, polling 126,842 votes (43.9 percent) to 81,747

(28.3 percent) for Wilson and 80,326 (27.8 percent) for Simpson. He finished a distant third in New Orleans, where he polled only 17,000 votes, just 5,000 more than in 1923. He failed to win the state's second- and third-largest cities, Shreveport and Baton Rouge, but he amassed large totals in rural north Louisiana and did well in rural south Louisiana. Long carried 47 parishes, 38 of them by absolute majorities. Wilson defeated Simpson for second place on the basis of his totals in New Orleans.

Long's large lead created a psychological barrier to Wilson's ability to win a runoff. Money was unavailable to a likely loser; so were endorsements and volunteers. Long facilitated Simpson's decision to refuse to endorse Wilson by promises of jobs and also by dropping a pledge to investigate the Highway Commission for corruption. State and local politicians sprinted toward the Long bandwagon and jostled to leap aboard. The coup de grace occurred when the Old Regular caucus voted, on January 22, 1928, to remain neutral in a runoff. The next day Wilson announced his withdrawal. There was no meaningful campaign and only a perfunctory turnout for the general election in April. Long won 92,941 votes to 3,733 for the Republican opposition.

Long thus became governor without polling a majority of the primary vote. He benefited from the absence of unified opposition. This was the most honest, issue-oriented election that Louisiana experienced until 1940. Money, good weather, and the ineptness of his opponents contributed to his victory, as did his grass roots appeal.

Long had the temperament of a dissenter in the sense that he objected to the status quo, and in that he was inveterately dissatisfied with his station in life. He was a master improvisor, not a long-range thinker. As he achieved one goal, his ambition drove him to seek another. Huey always believed in his destiny; within weeks he began poring over books on Napoleon because a crackpot physician advised him that he was the French emperor reincarnated. He soon gave up; there were too many books and too little time. The night that Wilson conceded, Long told a band of revelers at the Roosevelt Hotel: "Stick by me.

We'll show 'em who's boss. I'm going to be president some day."

The Louisiana political and business establishment, which detested Long, had underestimated him, and now feared him, rushed to drown him in praise. There were still some minor ill feelings. New Orleans businessmen who sought funds to buy Huey a silver service refused to accept money from Maestri. Maestri took his money and bought Huey a diamond tiepin worth $2,500. Long accepted the silver set, although he complained that he did not know the purpose of many of the elegant utensils. He also began to wear diamond rings.

Gifts were not signs of mutual trust, however. Long's opponents grudgingly accepted him and wanted to buy him off. Long relished their humiliation. "No music ever sounded one half so refreshing as the whines and moans of the fat pie-eating politicians," he observed.

Long was inaugurated on May 21, 1928. The affair was the most unruly in memory. Some 15,000 citizens, including backwoods farmers, danced to hillbilly music and drank water from buckets with tin dippers. Long's address was brief, dull, and irrelevant to his subsequent actions. He said that he had no further political ambitions, would limit public spending, end waste, and make appointments on merit alone.

Even before his program materialized, his style attracted attention. Huey did not like the governor's mansion and lived in hotels. His family life was unconventional. Initially, Rose and the three children, Palmer Reed age 5, Russell age 8, and Rose age 10, moved into the mansion, where Huey also set aside a room for his mistress, Alice Lee Grosjean. Rose and the children soon moved back to Shreveport. Huey dispatched Grosjean to the Heidelberg Hotel, and Rose and the children returned. They departed again after Long rented a permanent suite at the Heidelberg, on the same floor as Grosjean. Huey also had a suite in the Roosevelt Hotel and lived in New Orleans when the legislature was not in session.

Long put dozens of relatives on the state payroll. The most lucrative position, inheritance tax collector in New Orleans, went to Earl. In return for agreeing to support Hugh Long and an ill sister, Huey paid Earl a salary nearly twice that of the governor. The position was one he had promised to abolish during his campaign; he vowed to use the money to build a hospital for tuberculosis patients near Lake Pontchartrain. Afterward, a New Orleans paper published Earl's photograph, with the caption: "New lakefront TB hospital."

Earl also served as Huey's surrogate. He was a valuable cog in the Long machine; Earl dealt with people better than Huey. He made friends whereas Huey dominated. Nonetheless, Huey did not trust Earl. "You have to watch Earl," he said. "If you live long enough he'll double-cross you." Earl also insisted on giving Huey unwanted advice. He did not seem to realize which Long was boss, Huey complained.

Huey never left any doubt as to who was boss. He said he would "rather be the biggest man in a little village than the second biggest man in a great city. Huey Long stands second to nobody." Political success magnified his arrogance. Stopped by a highway patrolman for speeding, he told the officer he was the governor, and was reprieving himself. Huey purchased a small library, chiefly biographies of great men. In a book about Benvenuto Cellini, he underlined two passages: "Know then, that men like Benvenuto, unique in their profession, stand above the law" and "Laws cannot be imposed on him who is the master of the law." In an advertising flyer for a book about Julius Caesar, Long underlined: "Julius Caesar built up a vast dominion by the force of his own personality."

Long acquired the nickname "Kingfish" shortly after he became governor. Huey and his cronies listened to the "Amos 'n' Andy" radio program. Long called an associate "Brother Crawford" and he called Huey "Kingfish." The name remained an inside joke until Huey used it publicly. He was dictating the terms of the sale of bonds to Highway Commission members in their negotiations with potential purchasers when one of the bidders challenged Long's presence on the grounds that the commission, not the governor, was authorized to set interest rates. "I am participating here anyway, gentlemen," Long insisted. "For the present, you can just call me the Kingfish." Long liked the name because it sounded important. He saved time answering the telephone because "when I picked up the receiver and said 'the Kingfish speaking,' everybody in Louisiana knew who was talking." Franklin Roosevelt always called Huey "Kingfish"; Long did not realize that Roosevelt considered it a joke.

Few Louisianans joked about Huey publicly. They feared he would humiliate them with sharp repartee or destroy them financially. Long kept a list of people he felt had wronged him; it included not only important people, but menial employees. Huey's threats were not idle and few risked the wrath of the Kingfish. Those who did lived to regret it.

Huey's control rested on a keen mind, bluff, bullying, and ruthlessness. He thwarted, embarrassed, and frustrated better educated men who challenged him. His friends marveled at his intellectual prowess; his enemies thought him fiendishly clever. Senator Richard B. Russell of Georgia, who knew many of the nation's leading politicians, told journalist Tom Wicker, "I believe that Huey Long was about the smartest man I ever knew." Had Long taken an IQ test, he probably would have scored in the genius range. With discipline and education, Long's mind could have made him a success in many fields. But he was neither disciplined nor educated. He borrowed ideas indiscriminately and he never admitted a mistake, delegated authority, or tolerated originality and independence. At caucuses and planning sessions he did nearly all the talking and he never realized that he could achieve more if he slowed down, planned carefully, collected details, and hired able assistants.

Long had no use for women in politics. His marriage was a tyranny, and he spent little time with his family. Nor was Grosjean his only extramarital affair. "Huey would get himself into trouble every now and then with some woman," a friend said. "Sure, he had relations and affairs with all kinds of women," Richard Leche told a Long biographer. "Once Maestri caught him in his office with Alice Lee Grosjean. He got a woman in trouble in New York and Seymour Weiss had to go up and pay $10,000. Once on a train a man invited Huey to his car. On the trip Huey assaulted his daughter. When reproached, he said 'You gotta try, don't you?'" Huey once offered to make an aspiring actress a star. "I think he could do it, but the first thing he would want to be in my pants," she said.

Huey did not attempt to charm or romance women, but sought merely to satisfy his sexual appetites. Sex was not his primary drive—power was—yet he was compulsive in everything and demanded immediate gratification. Even his closest friends found his eating habits obnoxious. Initially Long favored plain food. Until he became governor he was interested more in quantity than quality; he devoured whatever was available. Campaigning in Dry Prong, he munched canned Vienna sausage, sliced raw onion, and peanut brittle simultaneously. During one political crisis he ate strawberries and cream exclusively. He snatched food from friends and strangers. Because his bodyguards were present, the strangers rarely complained, and his followers knew this was a way to keep them in place. "In some ways he didn't act like a normal human being," a man who liked him said. "He would reach over and take your meal and eat it." Another friend remembered: "Once at a restaurant he ate my dinner. He was always doing things like that."

Long was abusive to waiters. He once swept a meal of oysters off the table, shattering dishes, because the oysters were prepared improperly. John Pinckney Brasheare once entered a Baton Rouge restaurant with Huey. Long demanded a steak with fried potatoes. Looking around, he saw a customer eating steak and potatoes, grabbed it off the table, and ate it, slapped down a $5 bill and ordered the cook to make another steak for the customer. Long also stuck his friends with bills. He carried little money and made his associates pay.

No moral or religious scruples inhibited Long's actions. He completely rejected his Baptist upbringing, but no man could pretend more to be a devoted churchman. The scriptural references in his speeches were neither spontaneous nor original. Huey hired an ex-preacher to lace his speeches with scripture. Campaigning, he was stuck in a small town on Saturday. A journalist asked Long where he intended to attend church the next day.

"Me go to church?" the Kingfish asked. "Why I haven't been to a church in so many years I don't know when."

"But you're always quoting the Bible," the reporter said.

"Bible's the greatest book ever written," Huey snapped, "but I sure don't need anybody I can buy for six bits and a chew of tobacco to explain it to me. When I need preachers I buy 'em cheap."

Many people expected Long to be an unconventional governor, but they were surprised by what occurred. By the beginning of 1930 Huey had altered state politics radically and administered shock therapy to a state accustomed to mild homeopathic remedies. In the process, he changed himself. He aroused high expectations and bitter animosity. He became a symbol for the end of an era and the dawning of a new one. In his rush he achieved unparalleled accomplishments through ruthlessness and political intuition. He also made mistakes in judgment and nearly succumbed to arrogance.

CHAPTER FOUR

Impeachment

❖
❖

At 34, Huey Long was the second-youngest governor in Louisiana's history. He knew little about the legislative process, viewing legislators as tools. Most lawmakers had supported Simpson or Wilson in the 1927 campaign; of 100 members of the House of Representatives, only 18 had backed Long; of 39 senators only 9 were Long men. Where a more seasoned politician would have employed finesse, Long was brutal. Although he made some strategic errors, Long's instincts were sound. He occasionally miscalculated the attitudes of legislators, but he understood the will of the common people. He also knew his power depended upon public approval, as well as money, allies, and patronage. While previous governors and Long's opponents seemed only dimly aware of this elemental principle of politics, Long never lost sight of it.

Whether motivated by greed and ambition or by genuine concern, he served his faction. Long did not try to achieve unanimous approval, alienated some potential backers and in the short run, behaved recklessly because he was undisciplined. But he focused on tangible accomplishments the public could comprehend, then publicized them. He considered image more important than substance and, therefore, built monuments to himself, partly from vanity, but also because he was a shrewd politician.

He set out to manufacture a legislative and popular majority, creating an economic and political elite attached to his machine, advancing irresistibly. Public contracts constituted one enticement. He tamed interest groups with rewards and threats. The threats were not idle; the rewards were not meager. "If you were for him, you could have anything," Edward A. Haggerty said. "If you were against him, God help you unless you were an extraordinary man."

Cecil Morgan, who led the movement to impeach Long, observed, "He was as cold-blooded in his desire for power as a human being could be." And an angry widow, Mrs. Clarence Pierson, recalled that her husband lost his state job for not giving money to Long as the poor man lay dying of cancer. Long not only employed such tactics, he relished them. Julius compared previous corruption to his brother's as "a mouse to an elephant." Huey told friend Gene Austin, "I want power so that I can do all the things I want to do. Give me that militia and they can have all the laws they want."

Long benefited from the chaos of state politics. Most interests and many legislators were ready to tilt toward the political wind. A handful of legislators, most of whom believed the end did not justify the means, opposed Long on principle. Long imagined his opposition larger than it was, and misjudged its motives. These adversaries did not blindly oppose everything Long proposed, nor were they monolithically conservative. They lacked a leader and constituted a loose coalition rather than a stable faction. Some simply did not like to be ordered around. Norman Bauer of St. Mary Parish said he fought Long because of "his overbearing ways." During his first legislative session Long warned Morgan, of Caddo, that if he voted against the highway bond issue, Long would fire his father, a state bank examiner. Morgan voted no, and his father was fired.

J. Y. Sanders, Jr., a state representative from Baton Rouge, represented a constituency dependent upon Long's archenemy, the Standard Oil refinery. His father was a prominent Long opponent, and he disliked Long's arrogance. Nonetheless, he respected Huey's ability and voted for some of his programs. He supported Long's bill to provide free textbooks but opposed the method of financing them. Edmund E. Talbot, who had known Huey since they were teenagers, said: "I never felt I could trust Huey. He lacked firm moral fiber. I was afraid of him, afraid to go with him."

Long's first legislative objective was to place his supporters in key positions. He sponsored the election of John B. Fournet as speaker of the House and Phillip H. Gilbert as president pro tempore of the Senate, then stacked every committee. The ultimate insult occurred when Long excluded Old Regulars from seats on the Committee on Orleans. Legislators from outside the city would dominate the committee, which dealt solely with New Orleans.

Long aggressively seized patronage amounting to 25,000 jobs. He thought each state worker could deliver five votes to his machine, which gave him 125,000 votes in a state where about 300,000 cast ballots. Long also sought to manipulate parish and city jobs. For example, he gained control of the New Orleans Dock Board as well as the city's Levee Board and the Charity Hospital. The terms of the incumbents staffing some of these agencies did not expire in 1928, but Long discharged them anyway. The legislature enacted laws changing some terms and eliminating positions. The prerequisite for holding a state job was political loyalty. Furthermore, workers were forced to contribute to the Long campaigns; several months before elections they gave 5 to 10 percent of their paychecks to the machine. The funds were called "deducts," because the state deducted money from their salaries. The money was placed in a "deduct box" kept by Seymour Weiss. Huey boasted that it was an honest way to finance campaigns; his opponents used funds from special interests. However, the Long machine benefited from special interest money too, and it also extorted contributions. The way to obtain a state contract for buildings and highways was to bribe the person who awarded it. Contractors added the bribe to their bids; thus, the taxpayers paid.

Long did not deny that graft existed. When an *Atlantic Monthly* writer asked him about corruption in his highway program, he responded: "We got the roads in Louisiana, haven't we? In some states they only have the graft." Actually, many states had better roads, yet few had so many bribes. Most Louisianans did not complain. The roads were tangible, the graft unseen. Much of Long's program was financed by bonds, so he conveyed the impression that the roads were free. When the bills came due, neither the voters nor the politicians would be around to pay them. Continued by Huey's heirs, these policies bankrupted the state. The deficit stimulated the economy during the Depression, but Louisiana's credit rating eventually fell so low that bonds could no longer be sold.

Whatever the long-range repercussions, Longism produced results. Huey not only proposed creative legislation, he guided it through the legislature. Stalking the floor of the House and Senate, he shouted instructions on how to vote. Long sent administration bills to stacked committees, barged into meetings and took over. As the committee chair sat mute, he explained bills and called for votes. The chairman banged his gavel, a bill passed, and Long turned to another one. "I'd rather violate every one of the damn conventions and see my bills passed than sit back in my office, all nice and proper, and watch 'em die," he rationalized. He compared the legislature to a deck of cards. "A deck has 52 cards," he boasted. "I hold the deck and I will deal it myself. In the legislature, I can have bills passed or kill them."

Long's pledge to pipe cheap natural gas to New Orleans was the first promise he fulfilled. However, he compelled New Orleanians to pay more than necessary. Bills were pending to require the New Orleans Public Service Commission, Inc. (NOPSI) to permit use of its pipelines at the cost to consumers of 80 cents per thousand cubic feet of natural gas. Long promised 70-cent gas during the campaign, and the company asked only 65 cents. Inexplicably, Long killed the 80-cent bill and backed one providing 95-cent gas, plus a 25-cent meter fee. Long protected the company's profits at the expense of consumers. Most New Orleanians, unaware of the deals cut, were glad to have gas.

The accomplishment that most endeared Long to poor Louisianans was free textbooks for elementary and secondary students. The idea had been conceived by Mrs. Harley Bozeman of Winnfield. Supporting the campaign of J. S. Porter, a local druggist running for parish representative in 1923, she printed 3,000 circulars promoting Porter as an advocate of free books, and gave Huey 25 circulars to distribute. Long liked the idea and adopted it during his own campaign. Neither Porter nor Long won but Long campaigned for free books again in 1927.

Long faced two questions: Would he give books to parochial as well as public schools, and how would he pay for them? Huey knew his plan would be unpopular with Louisiana Catholics if he limited books to public schools. His bill, therefore, made the books available to all students. North Louisiana Baptists opposed this, yet there were fewer Baptists than Catholics. Long solved the revenue problem by increasing the severance tax on natural resources by taxing volume rather than value. This placed a burden on his arch foe, Standard Oil.

Long's plan was challenged in court. Bossier Parish sued on the grounds that parishes and local school boards should set policy for textbooks. A judge who ruled the parish had no standing as a litigant dismissed the suit. Caddo Parish sued on the grounds that providing books to parochial schools violated the separation of church and state. Long fought this suit to the United States Supreme Court, where he won by arguing that the books were for *students,* not *schools.* The plan was also imperiled by a suit by oil companies that challenged the severance tax. Courts ruled the tax could not be collected while the case was being tried, so Long had to find interim financing. He received permission from the Board of Liquidation to borrow $500,000 from Louisiana banks but the bankers refused, arguing that the loan required legislative approval. Huey told them that the state owed their banks thousands of dollars; he would refuse payment unless the new loans were approved. The bankers agreed to more loans, although they were correct in arguing that the loan was illegal.

Long promised in 1927 to build surfaced highways to replace dirt and gravel roads. Louisiana had only 296 miles of concrete and 35 miles of asphalt roads outside the cities. Rural northern Louisiana was particularly isolated. The rudimentary system was not due to state neglect so much as to the limited numbers of automobiles. Long's governorship coincided with the automotive revolution. When the 1920s opened there were only 3 million automobiles in the United States; by 1930 there were 23 million. Louisiana got automobiles later than most states; few cars were seen outside of New Orleans before the late 1920s. In 1920 there were just 73,000 automobiles in Louisiana, but by 1924 there were 178,000. Long exploited the demand and took credit for pulling Louisianans out of the mud.

Huey's program was popular because he financed it largely by borrowing rather than by taxing. He began by submitting legislation authorizing $30 million in highway bonds. Because the Louisiana constitution prohibited such bond issues, a constitutional amendment requiring a two-thirds approval of the legislature and a popular referendum was necessary. The bill passed easily and was approved by voters in November, 1928. A small increase in the gasoline tax secured the bonds.

Long's ambitious highway program included bridges. By 1932, 10,000 construction workers were building highways; these jobs were badly needed during the Great Depression. Long gave the people a taste of roads, whetting their appetite for more and inducing the legislature to approve larger bond issues. The first roads were fragments of a system, short stretches of pavement followed by long gaps. Long admitted that politics determined construction. "We had started on the paved road system by scattering the work through the parishes, putting five or fifteen miles to the parish," he wrote. "When the people once knew the pleasure of traveling over paved highways their support for a program to connect up the links was certain."

The quality of the roads was poor, the price inflated, and the program riddled with corruption. In return for bribes, contracts went to political supporters, who charged more than the market value for materials. Longite Joseph Fisher sold more than 50,000 cubic yards of clam shells to the Highway Commission at a rate double that on the open market. He concealed his profits by not reporting them on his income tax return.

O. K. Allen was appointed head of the commission so he could award contracts to Long's friends and deny them to enemies. Even more questionably, Allen, Long, and railroad and utility magnate Harvey Couch took over a failing Winnfield company that they reincorporated as the Louisiana Quarry Company. They received a $500,000 loan upon their guarantee to bankers that they would get public business. State engineers had rejected the company's rocks as too soft for highways, but this changed when the new owners took over. Louisiana Quarry charged the commission $1.65 per ton for crushed rock while better quality rock was available for 62.5 cents. To further pad the bill, they watered the crushed rock to increase its weight. Highways that cost the state $45,000 to $50,000 per mile could have been built at a cost of $7,000 to $9,000. Because Long wanted to pad mileage statistics, the highways were narrower than those in other states. Long's highways were never more than 18 feet wide, although 22 feet is the safe minimum. No drainage was provided, no foundations were laid, slabs were poured directly onto the ground, and erosion washed roads away. Not much money went to maintenance; Long left the problem of repairing the poor roads to future governors.

In the short run, though, Long's highways were enormously popular and the people demanded more. The highways, textbooks, and natural gas for New Orleans were tangible accomplishments that no quibbling over cost or quality could challenge. Long added to his power by sponsoring a bill creating the Bureau of Criminal Identification, which became a law enforcement agency for the governor, independent of state or municipal police forces. He vindictively vetoed appropriations for the Public Service Commission, now controlled by his enemies. Huey did not get everything he wanted, for example, a court-packing plan to expand the number of state appellate judges with the governor appointing the new ones.

Long flaunted the law to raid gambling in parishes surrounding New Orleans. Few governors had attempted to control gambling but Long decided to raid gambling establishments to impress his fundamentalist constituents who considered gambling sinful and to compel the gamblers to pay for protection. In August and November of 1928 and again in February of 1929 he raided gambling houses in St. Bernard and Jefferson parishes without using the state police or obtaining search warrants, illegally surprised and searched wealthy patrons, and confiscated cash. Long did not intend to prosecute the gamblers because the guardsmen burned evidence and the cash disappeared. When Attorney General Percy Saint declared the raids illegal, Long replied, "Nobody asked him." Eventually Long stopped the raids. "If you folks down here are just born gamblers, I guess there's nothing I can do to stop you," he declared in 1935.

The February, 1929, raid proved politically embarrassing. That evening Huey attended a French Quarter party thrown by his friend, Alfred Danziger. The governor flirted with women and got drunk, confiding to them that the National Guard would raid specific gambling establishments later that night. One woman warned the proprietors, so when the Guard arrived gambling had stopped. Guests at the Danziger party testified about the governor's behavior that night at his later impeachment hearings.

In the November 6, 1928, election Louisianans voted for president. The Democratic candidate, New York Governor Al Smith, and the Republican nominee, Secretary of Commerce Herbert Hoover, both had large followings in Louisiana. Hoover, a Quaker, drew Protestant support, and Smith, a Catholic, inspired the loyalty of Louisiana Catholics. Hoover was an underdog in Louisiana; it was the only southern state with a majority of Catholic voters and had voted Democratic in every presidential election since 1876. Louisiana delegates to the Democratic national convention had supported Smith for the nomination. Long wanted to remain neutral but Colonel Ewing persuaded him that he could not expect patronage from the Democratic Party if he did not support Smith. Delivering several speeches for Smith during the waning days of the campaign, Long denounced bigots who would vote against a Catholic because of his religion, but added that he did not think it appropriate to elect a Quaker. He also raised the specter of white supremacy, warning that Hoover's election meant "negro [sic] domination or social equality." He added, "We believe this is a white man's country and are not willing to turn it over to the negroes." Whether motivated by fear of black Republicanism or empathy for a fellow Catholic, Louisianans gave Smith his largest statewide majority in the nation. The country elected Hoover.

Long summoned a six-day special session of the legislature after the election in December to implement his road program. He also used the session to compel Caddo Parish to accept free textbooks. Shreveport was anti-Long and its mayor, Lee Thomas, hated Huey. The legislative delegation, which had voted against the books, quickly learned that an angry Kingfish was dangerous. The Army Air Corps wanted to construct an air base near Shreveport that would add $5 million annually to the local economy, but needed state permission to acquire the land. Huey refused to put a bill authorizing the transfer into his call for the session. When the Shreveport delegates complained, he said they must accept the books if they wanted the airport. Asked if he had coerced Caddo, Long replied: "I didn't coerce them. I stomped them into distributing the books."

Because the session determined priorities for highway construction, the Caddo delegation requested funds for local roads. The Kingfish replied that the lawmakers would be lucky to see a state concrete mixer if they continued to defy him. "Caddo Parish has to get right before it can get a damned thing out of this administration," he said. "I will teach you to get off the sidewalk, take off your hat, and bow down damn low when Governor Long comes to town."

Huey considered the governor's mansion rundown, unsafe, and termite-infested and he wanted a new one as a showcase for his administration. Again, Long was in such a hurry that he bypassed the legislature. The Board of Liquidation authorized $150,000 to construct a mansion, subject to legislative approval. Long had convicts from the state penitentiary demolish the mansion.

Huey felt invulnerable. A month later he broke with Sullivan and Ewing, his 1927 New Orleans allies, and with his lieutenant governor, Paul Cyr, believing he no longer needed their support. Ewing and Sullivan had not delivered the vote in New Orleans and were unlikely to be effective in future campaigns. Ewing welcomed the break. He considered Huey's gambling raids atrocities and the searches that accompanied them humiliating. Ewing and Cyr wanted Long to commute the death sentence of a woman convicted of murdering her husband. Louisiana had never hanged a white woman, they argued. The key to the split, however, was not any specific issue, but that these men gave Long unwanted advice. Cyr harbored another grievance: He asked Long to support him for governor in 1932, since the Kingfish could not succeed himself, and Huey refused. The breaks proved harmful, but not fatal, to Huey's career. Within months, he would need allies and Cyr would be in a position to hurt him.

Long's troubles began when the Supreme Court declared his severance tax unconstitutional. Because the tax was to fund textbooks, the governor needed an alternative revenue source to continue the program. Therefore, he called a special session of the legislature to meet for six days, beginning March 18, 1929. His agenda for the session included revision of the flawed severance tax and imposition of a five-cent-per-barrel tax on refined oil.

Long's success had convinced him that his program would win approval easily. Precisely the opposite happened. When the session opened, the rabbi who delivered the invocation refused to ask for God's blessing for "such a governor." Many legislators considered the oil tax unwise and unnecessary, and the business community opposed it. Furthermore, they thought Long was punishing Standard Oil. The Baton Rouge economy relied upon the refinery, and Huey, who had never won an election in Baton Rouge, wanted to hurt the corporation and the community.

By attempting to force through the oil tax, Long galvanized his opponents and destroyed the legislative majority he had created in 1928. Many legislators who personally disliked Huey had voted for his program because they knew it was popular; now they could openly oppose him on an issue that the public also opposed. Long quickly discovered his miscalculation. His bills could pass in the short session only if he could muster a two-thirds majority to suspend the rules. He could not command so large a majority, and his support dwindled on every vote. In a longer session he would not need to suspend the rules. Huey, therefore, summoned an 18-day session to assemble on the afternoon of March 20 after adjournment *sine die* (permanently) of the 6-day session that morning.

Yet Long's prospects did not improve. The House ordered the sergeant-at-arms to enforce the rule barring unauthorized visitors and Long was ejected from the floor. Resolutions condemned the oil tax, called for investigations of the Highway Commission, and demanded that Long account for funds spent without authorization. Earlier Long's opponents had tried to adjourn to thwart passage of his program; now Long wanted to adjourn to avoid embarrassment but the opposition insisted on remaining in session.

Every night the two sides caucused. Some foes suggested that they use the anger at the governor to impeach him. They had received reports of vote-buying, graft, and illegal activities. Battling Bozeman (no relation to Harley Bozeman), the Kingfish's former bodyguard, asserted that Huey had ordered him to murder Representative J. Y. Sanders, Jr., in return for money and clemency. Bozeman agreed to swear to his accusation in an affidavit that Morgan would read on the House floor.

While the anti-Longs caucused, Huey's support declined. Cyr charged the governor with helping cronies earn millions by leasing them state oil land for a fraction of its value. After the New Orleans *States* published a list of "double dippers," legislators who voted with the administration in return for jobs, the Senate adopted a resolution condemning vote-trading. Newspapers reported that the governor had given contracts for state refrigeration equipment to his friend W. K. Henderson without competitive bidding and that he had paroled a convict illegally. Editorials in the Baton Rouge *State-Times* so angered Long that he warned its publisher, Charles Manship, that if he continued the governor would reveal that Manship's brother was hospitalized in a state mental institution. Outraged, Manship responded with a front-page editorial, "This, Gentlemen, is the Way Your Governor Fights."

For the first time since becoming governor, Long was frightened; he had lost control. On March 24, he instructed his

House leaders to move for adjournment when the House convened the next day. The House opened with a roll call. Afterward, several representatives demanded the floor, yet Speaker John B. Fournet, as instructed, recognized Representative Cleveland Fruge, who moved adjournment *sine die.* Simultaneously, Morgan rose on a point of personal privilege. Despite Fournet's attempts to silence him, Morgan continued, "I have in my hand an affidavit from a citizen of Baton Rouge that the governor has tried to procure the assassination of a member of this House!" Fournet ordered the sergeant-at-arms to seat Morgan, but Morgan's friends prevented that. "I propose to have my say here and not one of you will shout me down," he said. He continued to read the affidavit.

Bedlam reigned; Fournet requested a vote on the motion to adjourn. Representatives rushed to press the buttons that recorded their votes. However, the electronic voting machine did not register the votes accurately. An overwhelming majority voted to remain in session, but the machine showed 79 for adjournment and only 13 against. Legislators shouted that the vote was fixed. Fournet declared the House adjourned *sine die* and walked out.

Legislators began fighting; one received a bloody nose from brass knuckles. Spectators rushed from the galleries to join the melee. Representative Harney Bogan seized the gavel and banged it for order; no one listened. Then Mason Spencer, in a booming voice, took the chair and demanded order. From the confusion on the floor a voice of reason rang out. "Point of order!" yelled Representative George J. Ginsberg. "A motion to adjourn *sine die,* as this was, is unconstitutional. The constitution provides that no house can adjourn for more than three days without the consent of the other house."

Ginsberg was correct: The vote was irrelevant. A motion to appeal the decision of the chair carried 71–9. The House remained in session but was in no condition to do business, and the weary, bloody legislators agreed to adjourn until the morning after the affair that journalists called "Bloody Monday."

The next day, Fournet returned to the speaker's chair and apologized for leaving, yet denied that the voting machine was rigged. Longites claimed they did not fix the vote; the machine had not cleared from the previous roll call. It is highly unlikely, however, that 13 representatives would have voted "no" on a roll call. Whether or not the Longs rigged the machine, they must have realized that the vote Fournet accepted was incorrect; it was clear that a majority wished to remain in session. Some demanded Fournet's impeachment but the opposition could not unite. The speaker's fate seemed minor compared to the issue at hand: the impeachment of Long. A copy of a petition citing 19 charges of impeachment was on every representative's desk. The charges included every reason for impeaching a governor except habitual drunkenness; some wanted that included too. The Louisiana press also demanded impeachment.

Long was frightened. An aide found him sobbing in bed, "They've got me." The usually talkative governor had nothing to say to reporters. Still, those who thought he would concede misjudged Long. "Always take the offensive," he once advised a young politician. "The defensive ain't worth a damn." He decided to appeal to the people.

Long needed money and time. Robert Maestri gave $40,000; his opponents provided the time. Huey believed his best hope lay in persuading legislators that if they voted to impeach their constituents would defeat them. He depicted himself as a martyr persecuted by Standard Oil. Long also profited from a provision in the state constitution that permitted the governor to remain in office during impeachment proceedings, which enabled Huey to use patronage in his defense. Without it Cyr would have become acting governor and utilized the powers of the office to convict Long.

Most people, who did not anticipate Long's spirited defense or the ineptitude of his enemies, believed the impeachment movement would succeed. "It was," H. L. Mencken wrote, "a battle to the death between gorillas and baboons." In fact, what transpired during the month that followed resembled a circus more than a legislature.

Neither side had time to prepare a thoughtful presentation; both made tactical errors and acted unethically. Some would vote for conviction or acquittal regardless of the evidence. Long bought votes with patronage; his opponents bought them with money. Most legislators, however, made their decisions on political grounds. A majority favored conviction, but not the two-thirds majority needed for a Senate conviction.

Huey's defense team included nine attorneys who met daily to devise strategy. Desperate, they pursued strategies that led down blind alleys before discovering one that worked. One supporter, Representative George Delesdernier of Plaquemines Parish, argued that a special session could not impeach Long because impeachment was not among the items listed for consideration in the governor's call for the session. "Do you think," a Long opponent responded, "that the governor would ever call a special session to impeach himself?"

The prosecution was yet more inept. Testimony, much of it irrelevant, was introduced in no specific order, skipping from one charge to another. The impeachers had no timetable for voting on charges. Time wasted played into the hands of the Longites. The charges, not carefully drawn, constituted a mixture of trivial and serious accusations; for example, witnesses testified that Long had used profanity. The prosecution would have been more effective if it had focused on a few charges and documented them extensively. Conviction on just one count would remove Long from office and disqualify him from running again.

Testimony began on April 3, just three days before the legislative session was due to end, according to the governor's call. The House first heard testimony that Long bought votes in the legislature by offering state jobs. Representative Adolph Geymard said Long offered to cancel a $25,000 debt Geymard owed the state and to give him his choice of three lucrative state jobs if he would vote with the administration. Asked if he considered the offers a bribe, he responded, "Yes sir, I do." Representative Davis Richarme testified that he had been at a meeting at which the governor offered Representative Felix Delaune a job in return for his vote; Delaune accepted the job and began voting Long's way. Sheriff C. H. Andrews of East Feliciana Parish testified that Long had boasted about bribing representative W. H. Bennett, "I bought and paid for him like you would a carload of potatoes." The defense argued that the governor was joking. "I don't remember if he smiled, but I took it that he meant it," Andrews replied. A second witness also agreed that Long was serious.

Without voting on the bribery charge, the House considered the accusation that Long had tried to blackmail Manship using his brother's mental disability. The defense argued that state records were public documents, but the prosecution countered that medical records of patients in state hospitals had been specifically exempted from the Public Records Act of 1912. The defense shifted tactics and argued that Long's threat, which he did not deny, had not been made in his capacity as governor. The prosecution might have argued that blackmail was grounds for impeachment regardless of the circumstances. Furthermore, the editorials Long wanted to stop concerned his administration, not his private life. However, the prosecution dropped the matter.

After the House adjourned in the evening Long staged a rally to promote his defense. Huey did not attempt to refute the charges against him; rather, he attacked the credibility of his opponents. He claimed that Standard Oil had inspired the impeachment and was bribing legislators to convict him. The issue, he said, was not his actions, but the special interests versus the people.

Long flooded the state with millions of circulars distributed by Highway Commission trucks and State Police cars, attacking his opponents. "I had rather go down to a thousand impeachments," he wrote, "than to admit that I am the Governor of the State that does not dare to call the Standard Oil Company to account so that we can educate our children and care for the destitute, sick, and afflicted." Standard had mobilized enough money to "burn a wet mule" in its attempts to bribe legislators. "Watch out for the lying newspapers. Pay no attention to anything they say," he warned.

Long's tactics infuriated his opponents. The legislature passed resolutions calling upon Long to submit the names of those who had offered bribes and those who took them. He admitted he had no evidence, but did not stop the accusations. Other opponents argued that if he were innocent, Huey would refute the charges rather than deliver speeches. "Nineteen serious charges have been lodged against the governor," the Baton Rouge *State-Times* wrote. "He is at perfect liberty to discuss those charges; no one has muzzled him. But he has not chosen to discuss them."

The hearings dragged on until April 25. On April 4, Seymour Weiss testified reluctantly about charges that Long had purchased a private automobile with funds appropriated to entertain a convention of governors. The evidence was circumstantial: Huey could not explain how he had obtained so much cash on short notice, the bills he used to buy the car were the same denomination Weiss had used to pay bills for the conference, and Weiss refused to account for $2,000. He said he used cash exclusively because writing checks was too much trouble. He obtained receipts for the expenditures, but he and Huey burned them. Weiss claimed money had been spent for a party with liquor and women, but governors who had attended claimed that no such party had taken place. The legislature, which could have punished Weiss for contempt, did not, nor did it resolve the mystery of the money.

Long was accused of misappropriating other state funds. He admitted using maintenance funds for the governor's mansion to purchase a personal law library; the money was not needed for the mansion because he had torn it down. Moreover, the mansion's contents had disappeared and Long refused to account for them. Officials testified that Huey had paid for defective culverts for drainage projects because a crony did the work. He had friends and relatives on the payroll who did not work. As evidence, the prosecutors summoned Joe Messina, a bodyguard, cook, and valet for Long. The following exchange took place between Messina, whom the Highway Commission paid as a license inspector, and a prosecutor:

"What department were you in at the Highway Commission?"

"I don't know."

"To whom did you report?"

"I was not told to report to anyone."
"Do you know the license law?"
"No."
"How much license money did you turn in?"
"None."
"What violations did you find?"
"None."
"Did you ever read the law?"
"No, but I could tell a 1928 from a 1929 license."

On April 6 the House voted 58–40 to impeach Long on the Manship blackmail charge. The vote was equivalent to a grand jury indictment; conviction would require a two-thirds majority of the Senate. It was now certain that a Senate trial would occur, but the House heard testimony for three more weeks before adjourning.

An incoherent speech in defense of Long by Delesdernier compared the impeachment to the crucifixion. "Bear with me in patience while I say what I have to say," he began. "The title of my speech will be 'The Cross of Gold and with Shackles of Paper.' Nineteen hundred years ago there was a cross of wood erected and a Divine Creature of that time was nailed to the cross. This Divine Creature was going through the country relieving the sick and afflicted, curing the lame and the halt, aiding the deaf and the blind, and driving illiteracy from the country that surrounded Him to teach salvation to man, woman and child. He was surrounded by a committee of twelve. There was a traitor in the ranks. Charges were preferred before a judge." Cries of "Blasphemy!" arose in the chamber. One representative moved that the rule against sacrilegious statements in the House be invoked, but Delesdernier said he had not specifically mentioned Jesus. He continued: "Today there is a creature relieving the sick and the blind, aiding the lame and the halt, and trying to drive illiteracy from the state, and he is being shackled with paper to a cross."

By now protests were so loud that Delesdernier could not continue. Perhaps carried away by his own oratory, he fainted. Friends splashed water in his face and carried him to a window; he recovered in time to vote no on the Manship charge. A journalist called the oration the most ridiculous ever delivered by a Louisiana legislator. If so, it is quite an accomplishment, considering the competition.

Interrupted by such digressions, the hearings proceeded slowly. The first bill of impeachment passed April 6, the next on April 11, and the final one not until April 26. The Senate remained in session, awaiting conclusion of the House proceedings.

Much of the testimony related to corruption. Several state officials testified that Long had hired and fired employees regardless of the law or their qualifications. A Baptist minister testified that he had seen Long carry a pistol beneath his coat. "Don't you know," a Long defender argued, "that the governor is commander-in-chief of the state militia?" An opponent responded, "If you can find where that authorizes him to carry a concealed weapon, I'll buy you a new suit of clothes!" Dr. V. L. Roy, who had been president of the State Normal School for 18 years, testified that Long forced him to resign because he refused to campaign for him during a referendum on constitutional amendments. "On election day," Roy said, "the governor called me on the telephone and told me that one of the ballot boxes near the State Normal School 'wasn't going right' . . . to go out and get busy. I was incensed. I never heard such a request being made of a college president."

On April 11, the *Morning Advocate* revealed that Long already had commitments from 15 senators to vote against conviction; they had signed a round-robin. Although the story was true, Long denied it and embarked on a tour to rally public support. With the round-robin secure in his safe, Huey's public rallies were superfluous, although perhaps he wished to prevent the signers from wavering and persuade the prosecution that their case was hopeless. During one speech he attacked Gilbert Dupre, a 70-year-old legislator, who was hard of hearing. "Some people claim to be honest just because they are deaf," he said. The old man retorted, "I certainly never before heard of a man who would ridicule another man's infirmity."

The hearings reached a nadir of irrelevancy on April 25, with testimony about Long's activities at the party hosted by

Danziger. Danziger said women entertainers wearing grass skirts had danced the hula, and one of them sat on Huey's lap. The entertainer, Helen Crawford, was called to testify. "Everybody was drunk," Crawford said, "and the governor had plenty." She added that he had staggered around and tried to dance with the women, and that she had indeed sat on his lap. The defense quickly moved to raise doubts about her credibility.

"Now little miss, aren't you accustomed to sitting on men's laps?"

"I am not," Crawford responded.

"Have you ever sat on a man's lap?"

Despite prosecution objections, the question was permitted. Legislators leaned forward to hear her reply.

"Yes," Crawford conceded. "I am married."

The charge that had provoked the impeachment attempt—Huey's offer of money to Bozeman to assassinate Sanders—never reached a vote. No one denied that Long had made the offer, but his defenders insisted he was drunk, his opponents that he was sober. Bozeman testified that both sides were correct: Long had initially made the offer while drunk, then repeated it when sober.

During the last day of testimony, April 26, Earl Long spotted Maestri talking with an enemy, Representative Bogan, outside the House chamber. "Why are you talking to this son of a bitch?" Earl demanded. Bogan responded by punching Earl and they tumbled to the floor. Before they could be separated, Earl bit Bogan on the ear. Bogan sought medical attention and took an injection of tetanus serum, returning to the House in time to vote on the final bill of impeachment.

Of the 19 bills, 9 were adopted, 1 was defeated, and 9 were dropped without a vote. The more serious charges passed were that Huey attempted to blackmail Manship, misappropriated money intended for the governor's conference, bought law books with state money, bribed members of the legislature, illegally fired a state employee, paid relatives and friends public money for personal services, and was incompetent and temperamentally unfit for office.

The Senate received the charges, then adjourned until May 15, when the trial began. Because conviction required a two-thirds majority, the votes of 14 of the 39 senators could thwart it. On opening day, the defense offered two demurrers claiming the charges were technically flawed and therefore invalid. The first demurrer failed narrowly. The second demurrer claimed the Manship charge, the only one voted on before April 6, was invalid because it was a private act. This demurrer passed 21–18. It was clear from the votes that the prosecution lacked the two-thirds majority necessary to convict.

The next day, after the opening roll call, Senator Phillip H. Gilbert asked the Senate secretary to read a motion to dismiss all charges. The motion, signed by 15 senators, more than one-third of the body, stipulated that the signers would vote against impeachment because the remaining bills of impeachment had been adopted after April 6, the adjournment date set in the governor's call. The chair polled each signer, who attested to the authenticity of the document and his commitment to oppose conviction. The other senators caucused, conceded that further prosecution would be futile, and accepted a motion to adjourn *sine die*. Long had defeated the most serious challenge to his power he would ever face. However, by adjourning without a vote, the charges stood and could be revived and passed by a later legislature. Furthermore, Long could not claim innocence because his guilt or innocence had never come to a vote. Even some Long supporters objected to terminating the trial without hearing the evidence. In addition to the 15 signers of the round-robin, 3 senators told Huey they would vote against each charge, but would not sign a round-robin pledge without hearing the evidence.

Long's brilliance lay not in conceiving the round-robin, which was not his idea, but in inducing senators to implement it. Each of the signers received a state job, a judgeship, or state contracts. Favors and public works, mostly road projects, were showered upon their constituents. On the other hand, Long punished the leaders of the impeachment movement. He initiated recall movements against nine legislators but none succeeded.

Long's enemies did not give up. In July, 300 of them met and created the Constitutional League to combat Long. Led by former Governor Parker, it raised $100,000 within 15 minutes. Its immediate objectives were to investigate corruption, revive the impeachment charges at the next session, and replace Speaker Fournet. Long dismissed them as the "Constipational League."

The prospect of opposition did not diminish the jubilation of the Long faction. Two weeks after the legislature adjourned Long took the Robineers to a Gulf resort for a party at which everyone, including Huey, got drunk. Although the narrow escape made Huey want to exterminate his opposition, it did not alter his basic character. "I used to try to get things done by saying 'please,'" he reflected later. "That didn't work and now I'm a dynamiter. I dynamite 'em out of my path."

The Kingfish regained his sense of humor. On March 30, 1930, a German cruiser, the *Emden,* docked in New Orleans and the commander made an appointment to meet Long in his suite at the Roosevelt Hotel. Formally attired, the commander and the German consul were ushered into Long's suite by Weiss. It was mid-morning, but the Kingfish had just arisen. He emerged from his bedroom, clad in silk pajamas, a robe, and slippers, exchanged pleasantries, then retired. Moments later Weiss returned to tell Huey that the Germans were furious because he had received them in pajamas. "What's the matter with them?" Huey responded. "I had on a pair of green pajamas, took the time to put on a pair of bedroom slippers, a $25 lounging robe given to me by the State Banking Department for Christmas— what more do they want?"

Huey apologized. He said he was sick and sleepy and just a poor Winnfield hick who knew nothing of diplomacy. "You see, I come from Winnfield up in the hills of Winn Parish, in this state," he said. Long visited the cruiser the next morning in formal attire. The incident gave Huey his first national publicity.

Huey learned to manipulate the press by buffoonery. However, he faced a serious challenge when the legislature convened in May 1930. The impeachment charges remained on the books. Furthermore, he had an ambitious program, which included a $75-million bond issue for highways and bonds for a new state capitol. When business interests made peace overtures, he accepted. In return for Long's shelving of occupational taxes on industry, the businessmen agreed to urge their state senators to vote to dismiss the bills of impeachment.

CHAPTER FIVE

Election to the Senate

❖
❖

Long knew the challenge to his power would resume when the legislature convened on May 11, 1930. He submitted to that session an ambitious economic program that included a $68-million bond issue to finance highways and bridges, a $5-million bond issue for a new state capitol, and modernization plans for the port of New Orleans. Long also had to turn back the attempt of the anti-Longs to replace John B. Fournet as House speaker, and the governor elected his candidate, Alvin O. King, president pro tempore of the Senate. Fournet and King, under instructions from Long, purged important committees of legislators who had tried to impeach Huey. The New Orleans delegation, all Old Regulars, led the opposition. The governor retaliated by persuading bankers to deny funds for New Orleans, forcing the city government to borrow from New York banks. Long was determined to destroy the Old Regular machine and the mayor elected in January, 1930, T. Semmes Walmsley, detested Long, whose attempts to bankrupt his city intensified his hatred.

The 1930 session was almost as unruly as the 1929 special session; fistfights erupted on the floor. Using patronage, threats, and promises, Long created a legislative majority but could not command the two-thirds majority necessary to approve constitutional amendments. The opposition harassed his administration by demanding an investigation into corruption. The Constitutional League furnished evidence to

Attorney General Percy Saint, who initiated a probe of the Highway Commission.

Realizing he could not enact constitutional amendments the governor submitted a bill to convene a constitutional convention to accomplish his objectives, which could be done by a simple majority. The bill passed the House 56–42 but Long's Senate foes filibustered to prevent a vote. Cyr, who presided over the Senate, helped the filibuster by permitting administration opponents to monopolize the floor. The legislature adjourned in July without enacting a single major Long bill.

Huey decided to appeal to the public. A month before his thirty-seventh birthday, he announced that he would challenge U.S. Senator Joseph E. Ransdell in the September 9 Democratic primary. He wanted the election to be a referendum on his administration: If he won, he would demand that the legislature enact his program; if he lost, he would resign as governor. It was a bold move that put his entire political career at stake. "Huey Long has piled all his chips on the table to bet on one throw of the dice," a journalist observed.

Because the major newspapers were hostile, Long founded the *Louisiana Progress*. Launched in March, 1930, it announced in the July 17 issue the Kingfish's candidacy, scooping the major dailies. For the remainder of Long's life, the *Progress* was the journalistic voice of his machine. Its history, financing, and publication schedule were chaotic; it ceased and resumed publication several times, and changed from a weekly to a monthly, then back to a weekly. After he decided to run for president, it became the *American Progress*. Within a year of its founding it claimed a circulation of 125,000, larger than that of any Louisiana daily, but the figure was doubtlessly inflated. The paper featured huge headlines in red and blue ink, and thoroughly partisan content. Long selected John D. Klorer, a New Orleans journalist, as editor, and hired cartoonist Trist Wood to ridicule his enemies. The cartoons, more malicious than humorous, were the most effective propaganda. Many of Long's constituents could not read but they did enjoy cartoons.

The *Progress* played a key role in Long's campaign for the Senate. One issue included an eight-column map of Louisiana showing highways Long would build if elected, "without one penny's increase in taxes." The *Progress* promised that the highway work "will be the greatest single step ever taken in the United States for state improvement." According to the paper, Long would build 1,000 miles of highways each year, and replace slow ferries with free bridges across major rivers.

Ransdell faced the full onslaught of Long's invective and patronage in one of the more vicious campaigns in Louisiana history. Long charged that Ransdell, at 71, was senile and ineffective, too old even to purchase life insurance. In fact, there were many congressmen and senators of Ransdell's age. Ransdell was neither brilliant nor vigorous, but he had influence in the Senate and he was effective in providing services to his constituents. Indeed, he obtained from the federal government more tangible benefits for the citizens of Louisiana than Long did as a senator, and perhaps he took some comfort in outliving his younger opponent by nearly 20 years.

Ransdell vainly attempted to compel Long to focus on national issues during the campaign. If Huey wanted to construct a highway system he could do so better as governor than as a U.S. Senator, Ransdell asserted. But Huey placed Ransdell on the defensive more often. Long claimed, for instance, that Ransdell had supported United States intervention in Latin America to protect the interests of New Orleans fruit magnate Samuel Zemurray. "Zemurray's gold is now poured out by the barrel to reelect Ransdell," Long claimed. The charge had no foundation in fact.

Long, who had helped to reelect Ransdell just six years earlier, had grown to detest him. Neither Ransdell nor Louisiana's other U.S. senator, Edwin S. Broussard, had supported Huey during the impeachment controversy. Ransdell had gone even further; he had joined the Constitutional League. Long's thirst for victory was so intense that he introduced the race issue into the campaign, reviving the accusation that Ransdell had addressed a letter to a black politician using the salutation "Mister." A copy of the letter was printed in the *Louisiana Progress* beneath the huge headline: "Ransdell's Political Love Letter to the Negro Walter Cohen." "Go to the polls and vote for the right of labor and for white supremacy—that means a vote against Joseph E. Ransdell," the *Progress* editorialized.

Long knew he commanded more grass roots support than the incumbent, who had been in Washington so long that people hardly knew him. But Long did not rely exclusively upon such support; he padded the payrolls before the election, particularly on the highway and conservation commissions. Employment at some of the smaller state agencies nearly doubled. Highway Commission engineers put out red flags in rural areas to show the location of paved highways to be built if Long won; farmers who wanted to move flags could do so. Government trucks and cars delivered millions of Long circulars and convicts at the state penitentiary painted campaign signs. State employees were assessed 10 percent of their salaries and were compelled to order from 10 to 50 subscriptions to the *Progress*, in which firms seeking state contracts bought advertising. Local leaders were told that if they expected to get roads in their parishes they must turn out the vote for Long. Official cars provided free transportation to the polls.

Huey manipulated the election machinery. In the campaign of 1927 Long had run as an outsider, relying on his personality, program, and wit to sway the electorate. Once in office, Huey represented a new order that he wanted to preserve at any cost. He did not trust free elections, and preferred to win a rigged election by a huge vote than to win a fair election by a modest margin.

Long perfected the use of "dummy" candidates. By law, each candidate for office submitted the names of an equal number of people to serve as poll commissioners who supervised voting and counted the ballots. The names were placed in a barrel and those drawn became the commissioners. The more candidates a faction ran, the better its chances were of having commissioners drawn. Long paid the filing fees for hundreds of candidates whose only purpose was to submit names to be drawn as commissioners. After the drawing, but before the election, the dummy candidates withdrew.

Long dramatically demonstrated his intention to win at all costs by kidnapping two political opponents, Sam Irby and

James Terrell, shortly before the primary. Irby, chief chemist for the Highway Commission, got his job through cronyism; he was the uncle of Long's mistress, Alice Lee Grosjean. But Irby was incompetent and dishonest and was fired. He developed a grudge against Long and sought revenge when state Attorney General Percy Saint investigated the commission. Irby voluntarily testified before a grand jury in Baton Rouge and said he could produce evidence that would embarrass the Kingfish. He drove to his home in New Orleans, intending to compile evidence, only to discover that his wife had left him to move in with Grosjean. He announced that he was going to Shreveport to file a slander suit against Long for alienating the affections of his wife. Grosjean's former husband James Terrell joined forces with his friend Irby, threatening to reveal lurid details of the Kingfish's affair. Irby and Terrell flew to Shreveport and checked into the Gardner Hotel. Foolishly, they informed Grosjean of their intentions and she immediately contacted Huey, who ordered agents of the Bureau of Criminal Identification to kidnap Irby and Terrell and hold them at remote outposts along Louisiana's Gulf Coast.

Shreveport journalists discovered the abduction five days before the primary and newsmen and the police launched a statewide search. Saint filed kidnapping charges against Long, and a hearing was set before a federal judge. Long told reporters that the men were being held in the Jefferson Parish jail for questioning about missing state documents. Reporters rushed to the jail but the men were not there. Then Long produced telegrams from Irby and Terrell addressed to relatives. One telegram allegedly written by Irby asserted: "I have no right to say anything about Governor Long. I know nothing about politics." Long also produced a telegram he claimed was a copy of one Terrell had written to his mother, addressed to Mrs. Norman. Long was unaware that the woman had remarried a few months earlier and used the last name of her current husband, Hasselroth, and the relatives denied receiving such communications.

The court postponed the hearing until after the election because material witnesses could not be located. Nonetheless, the scandal worried Long. In an effort to defuse the controversy he set up a statewide radio broadcast from his suite in the Roosevelt Hotel on September 7, two days before the primary. Irby, brought to Long's suite by armed guards, delivered a radio address written for him by Long, in which he professed friendship for the governor. Later he claimed that the bodyguards had held pistols to his head as he read.

After the election, Irby appeared in federal court and denied being kidnapped; no mention was made of Terrell, who had been freed previously. Because no witnesses could be found to testify to a kidnapping, the judge dismissed all charges. Subsequently Irby wrote a diatribe entitled *Kidnapped by the Kingfish,* in which he claimed that he had been taken by state officials, handcuffed, beaten, confined on Grand Island, and compelled to recite lies. Irby's credibility was dubious and bribes rather than threats may have induced his testimony. Nonetheless, the resources of the state clearly had been used to conduct the kidnapping and cover it up, and Long and others had committed perjury in federal court, grounds for removing him as governor and denying him a seat in the U.S. Senate. That such proof was not forthcoming reflected the fear and intimidation that pervaded Louisiana.

Long easily defeated Ransdell, polling 149,640 votes to the incumbent's 111,451. He had a huge lead in the rural parishes and lost New Orleans by less than 4,000 votes, winning 57 percent of the vote statewide. In addition, the Long machine won two congressional seats in the parishes surrounding New Orleans against candidates supported by Ransdell and the Old Regulars. Facing no opposition in the general election, Long, at 37, became a senator-elect.

Organized opposition collapsed. The day after the primary the Constitutional League dissolved. The Old Regulars surrendered and joined Huey's machine, agreeing to support his entire program, including dismissal of the impeachment charges. Long promised to appropriate $700,000 annually for street repair in New Orleans and to reserve $7 million of his highway bond issue for a Mississippi River bridge there. A special session of the legislature, which assembled on September 16, approved the entire program and the impeachment charges were dismissed. Long had not eradicated the opposition; he had absorbed it. He emphasized his ascendancy by appointing Grosjean, 24, secretary of state. Lacking experience or a college degree, she was unqualified by any standard except loyalty.

Huey remained a senator-elect rather than a member of the Senate for almost two years. Ransdell's term expired in March, 1931, but Long's gubernatorial term did not end until May, 1932. Huey had promised not to resign until a new governor was elected because he would not permit Lieutenant Governor Cyr to become governor. This meant that Louisiana would be represented by only one U.S. Senator for the interim. Long joked that he was only perpetuating the status quo; with Ransdell in office the state was unrepresented anyway.

Cyr argued that certification of the election returns made Long a senator even if he did not take his seat, and that Huey violated the provision in the state constitution that prohibited dual office holding. In October Cyr appeared before a Shreveport justice of the peace and took the oath of office as governor, intending to challenge Long's position. Unfortunately for Cyr, Long controlled the courts. Huey stationed troops around the capitol and the governor's mansion to bar Cyr and filed a countersuit accusing Cyr of dual office holding. Because he had taken the oath as governor, Long argued, Cyr was no longer lieutenant governor, and because his oath was illegal, he was not the governor. "Taking the oath of office as governor ends Dr. Cyr," Huey remarked. "He is no longer lieutenant governor, and he is now nothing."

The situation degenerated into farce. Long had Alvin O. King, the president pro tempore of the state Senate, sworn in as lieutenant governor and ordered Grosjean, his secretary of state, to pay the lieutenant governor's salary to King. On October 14, Mr. W. L. Aldrich of Shreveport appeared before a notary public and took the oath as governor, explaining that as long as the state appeared to have two governors there was no reason why it should not have three. A few days later two Shreveport men had themselves sworn in as lieutenant governor on the grounds that each of the governors deserved a lieutenant governor. Within days, taking the oath of office had become a fad in Louisiana. Notaries announced a reduced fee for swearing in aspirants.

Cyr unwittingly provided Huey with a pretext to destroy him. No state court would uphold Cyr's position, although it was at least as plausible as Long's. Eventually, the Louisiana Supreme Court ruled that it lacked jurisdiction in "one of the most bizarre decisions in American judicial history." The removal of Cyr permitted Long to resign as governor and take his seat in the United States Senate on January 25, 1932. King completed Huey's term.

While Louisianans were preoccupied by the Long impeachment proceedings and his subsequent comeback and entrenchment, the nation was fascinated and appalled by a stock market that soared to unprecedented heights in the fall of 1929, only to collapse in October. The crash was followed by a depression that dwarfed previous monetary crises. Millions of Americans lost their jobs, their homes, and their confidence. The plunge from prosperity to poverty transformed the political scene. Herbert Hoover, once praised as a humanitarian, became a scapegoat for Wall Street's failure; the Republican Party, which had dominated the politics of the 1920s, was blamed for the catastrophe.

The shadow of depression moved inexorably across Louisiana, whose people, once merely destitute, became desperate. The state's per capita income declined from $415 in 1929 to $222 in 1933. Urban Louisiana felt the shock of depression first but farmers were hit especially hard in a state that had only eight cities with populations above 10,000 in 1930, a state that relied on an agricultural economy. Farm income fell from $170 million in 1929 to $59 million in 1932. If farmers, who had not shared the prosperity of the 1920s, lost less than businessmen, it was because they had less to lose.

The Depression provided a favorable environment for Long's program of public works and deficit spending, although neither was a deliberate response to the collapse. State jobs became precious, patronage more potent. Long's election to the Senate provided him with the opportunity to transform himself from a regional curiosity to a national figure. Until taking his seat in Washington in 1932, however, he concentrated chiefly on state issues. He had earlier expressed little interest in higher education except to condemn his opponents for frivolous spending on Louisiana State University. By 1930 he had grown infatuated with LSU. A modest but growing university of 1,600 students in 1928, it received an "A" rating from a public accrediting association, an accomplishment for which Long claimed credit, even though he had nothing to do with it. But once he was no longer threatened with impeachment, Long broadened his interests. He realized that by making the state university a showcase he could promote himself and his state beyond Louisiana. He said he would take over LSU like "any other damned department."

When the university president resigned in 1930 and the board of regents wanted to hire a political enemy of Long's, he chose a president himself. He wanted an adequate but submissive person who would permit Huey to run LSU. Long found Dr. James Monroe Smith to be such a man.

Smith was neither ignorant nor incompetent, yet he was pliable and corrupt. He had received a B.A. from Valparaiso University, and a doctorate in education from Columbia University. Smith taught at Southwestern Louisiana Institute (now the University of Southwestern Louisiana) and became dean of the college of education in 1923. He realized he could advance his career by attaching himself and LSU to the Long organization. To do so, he had to accept Long's orders and public humiliation. Long recognized Smith's assets and limitations. "There's not a straight bone in Jim Smith's body," Huey said, "but he does what I want him to, so I think he's a good president."

Like many uneducated people, Long misunderstood academia. He was not so much interested in the content of education as in its pretensions: He regretted missing the undergraduate experience, which he perceived as football, fraternities, and carousing, not intellectual development. As in his quest for political power, his interest in higher education was compulsive, dictated more by his needs—especially the need for educated people to accept him—than by those of the students.

Long wanted academic glory through accomplishments that were rapid, tangible, and quantifiable. To him, quantity implied quality, manifested in large marching bands and more athletic scholarships, not intellectual freedom or a better library. In boasting of the music school, the only evidence he cited for quality was the number of grand pianos he purchased. He saw education as a tool to manipulate, not an experience to nurture, and did not comprehend that academic quality required time to incubate and did not always result in immediate payoffs.

Long thoroughly politicized higher education in Louisiana. His obsession with LSU created jealousy among other state colleges for which he did little. Even Huey's accomplishments at LSU were tangential to academic quality. He constructed only three buildings: a music school, a women's dormitory, and a field house. The million-dollar field house included a $500,000 swimming pool. After it was nearly completed, Long asked architect Leon Weiss if it were the longest pool in the country at 175 feet. Told that there was one pool that was a few feet longer, he ordered the workers to rip it up and extend it by seven feet. Contracts were awarded on the basis of cronyism and graft; the huge pool, for example, was completed before anyone noticed that the architects had neglected to include drains.

Long was determined to find money to finance his projects at LSU even without legislative approval. Rather than summon the legislature into special session, he diverted funds appropriated to the Highway Commission. Using money from the highway bonds and the bonds for a new Capitol, he arranged for the commission to pay $1.8 million to LSU for a parcel of land owned by the university to serve as the location for a new commission headquarters, and for the state to pay $350,000 for a second parcel of property for the site of the new capitol. "I'm the 'official thief' of LSU," he boasted.

Long also insisted on constructing a new medical school for LSU in New Orleans. At that time the only medical school in the state was at Tulane University. Huey claimed he wanted to provide a cheaper alternative to the high tuition charged at

Tulane, a private institution; he wanted a place where poor men and women from north Louisiana could become doctors. Huey personally planned each building. He announced the school in December, 1930; blueprints were completed by January, 1931; contracts let in March; construction began in April; and students started classes in October. Most Louisianans agreed that the state needed a medical school, but Long's opponents questioned locating it in New Orleans, far from the geographic center of the state. If Long's intention were to help poor people in north Louisiana, it would have been more logical to put the school in Shreveport or Alexandria. They attributed Long's determination to locate the school in New Orleans to a desire to punish Tulane for refusing to grant him an honorary degree.

During Long's regime the LSU faculty and the student body expanded. Enrollment grew from 1,600 in 1928 to more than 4,000 in 1933, yet the growth, not due entirely to his efforts, reflected a national trend during the Depression; as jobs evaporated, tuition costs declined, and federal aid increased. "It was cheaper for a student to come down here than to stay at home," a former dean explained. By 1933 more than one-half of the student body was on the state payroll. Unfortunately jobs were given not on the basis of need, but political loyalty. Furthermore, the largesse did not extend to students who attended other state colleges.

Long's initial interest lay in the university's band and its football team, for everyone could count the size of a band and the record of the team. Long's preoccupation with the band reflected his lifelong interest in music. Possibly the only time Huey relaxed was when listening to music. He enjoyed the dances at the Roosevelt Hotel and hired the director of the orchestra there, Castro Carrazo, to direct the LSU band, promising that as president he would make him Marine Band director. He wrote the words to some of Carrazo's compositions, including "Every Man a King." Long personally selected LSU majorettes and cheerleaders and sometimes marched at the head of the band during parades and football games. Without consultation, he demanded that President Smith create the largest band in the nation. In 1931 LSU spent only $837.57 on its law school and only $493.18 on its graduate school, but spent $14,345.65 on its band.

The LSU football team became a consuming passion. Long knew little about football. On the 11-man team at Winnfield High, he was the twelfth man, and never played in a game; asked what position he played, he replied "substitute." Initially he became a Tulane fan, but his allegiance shifted when the school refused to award him an honorary degree. Furthermore, it was located in the heartland of Long's opposition, many of its graduates were aristocrats who not only voted against Huey, but ridiculed his manners, and it had ties to the consistently hostile *Times-Picayune*. He belittled the elitism of private universities and developed a paternalistic affection for LSU.

In the early 1930s Huey appeared at practice nearly every day. Sirens blaring, his limousine roared up and parked on the field, where he watched the players scrimmage. He attended all the games, stalked the sidelines, sat on the bench, and entered the dressing room. Before one game with Arkansas, he delivered a pep talk. "Hell, you ought to beat 'em," he told the players. "We got better roads in Louisiana, free school books, and better everything." In the first half of the game LSU drove to the Arkansas 15-yard-line, but was penalized. At halftime Long summoned the referee to meet him under the stands. "You know who I am?" he said. "I'm Governor Long. If you want to penalize my boys do it out in the middle of the field, not near the goal line."

Long gave state jobs and perks to athletes. At halftime of the 1930 Missouri game, with LSU trailing, 6–0, Long told the players, "If you win, I'll give every slap damn one of you a job on the Highway Commission." Later, when one player told the governor he would like to make a little money, Huey peeled out a $100 bill and gave it to him. He brought players he liked to the governor's mansion and fed them gourmet meals.

"Huey had no conception of what the rules were," Fred Digby, a Longite, recalled. "On one occasion he told coach Russ Cohen that he had found a great player, Don Zimmerman, whom he would bring in. Cohen told Huey that Zimmerman was ineligible, having already played, and Huey, when he found that out, said that he would fire Zimmerman's father because the latter had promised that his son would play."

Long succeeded in making LSU a power but he was never satisfied. He hired coaches with a national reputation, entertained recruits lavishly, upgraded athletic facilities, and provided money to recruit. He hired Cohen, a respected coach, and the team improved. But the improvement was not rapid enough for Long, so he hired Biff Jones, one of the top coaches in the country.

Jones rejected an earlier offer from Huey and accepted in 1932 on the condition that Long refrain from interference. "Jones was a wonderful fellow, high class, and he resented it," Digby explained. "He knew that Huey didn't know any more about football than a rabbit knows about an airplane, but he was going to be a big man in front of everybody and tell everybody he was coaching the team." In three years under Jones LSU won 20 games, lost 5, and tied 6, establishing the highest winning percentage of any coach in LSU history. Still, it did not satisfy Huey. When in 1934 the Associated Press ranked the Tigers thirteenth nationally, Huey complained because they were not number 1. "If I conducted the poll and could pick my own election commissioners it would be different," he said.

At halftime of the final game in 1934, LSU trailed Oregon, 13–0. During the intermission Jones was diagraming plays in the dressing room when Huey arrived with a bodyguard and demanded to address the players. Jones told him that no one but he and his coaches could speak. "Who's going to stop me?" Long demanded. Jones, a towering ex-athlete, replied that he was. "All right, but you better win this one," Huey shouted. "I don't have to win this one," Jones replied. "Win, lose, or draw I'm going to resign at the end of this game." Years later, Jones remembered, "If Huey had talked two minutes and we'd won he would have thought he was responsible and he would have been in my hair like he was in Cohen's."

After Long departed, Jones told his players: "I've never asked a personal favor of you but I am now. I want to win this game more than anything else in the world." LSU won, 14–13, and Jones kept his promise to resign, going on to an outstanding coaching career at Oklahoma and Nebraska. Long could find no prominent coach who would accept his offers to succeed Jones and hired one of his assistants, Bernie Moore, whose teams compiled a mediocre record.

Long also put fans in the stands. He subsidized students who wanted to go to out-of-state games, sometimes by giving them money or by threatening railroads with increased tax assessments if they did not offer reduced fares to students. Once he invited students who wanted to attend a game at Vanderbilt to come to his hotel suite, where he handed out $20 bills as they filed by; one student collected three times, dressed in different clothes. When competition from the Ringling Brothers' circus threatened to reduce attendance at a home game, he made the circus perform in New Orleans rather than in Baton Rouge. If the circus management refused, he warned them, when they entered Louisiana from Texas he would enforce the state laws requiring dipping of animals to kill insects; they would have to dip elephants and tigers.

In 1934, J. Y. Sanders, Jr., who had been elected to Congress, resigned his seat representing Baton Rouge in the Louisiana Senate to go to Washington. As a joke, Long made his puppet governor, O. K. Allen, appoint LSU halfback Abe Mickal to the Senate. Huey dismissed objections that Mickal was underage, his voting residence was in Mississippi, and he was Syrian by birth. Mickal declined the honor.

Unfortunately the incident did not end there. An anti-Long student wrote a letter to the school newspaper, the *Reveille*, calling the appointment a "mockery of free political institutions." The student editors ran the letter, but Long learned of it and ordered 4,000 copies of the *Reveille* destroyed. Long also appointed a censor for the *Reveille* and ordered the editors to clear all material with her. The staff resigned over the censorship and 26 journalism students signed a petition supporting them. When the petition was printed in the Baton Rouge *State-Times*, Long ordered the staff and the signers suspended. The censor, Helen Gilkison, warned the students that they were jeopardizing their education. "You don't know what you're doing when you try to buck Huey Long," she cautioned. The students appealed to James F. Broussard, the dean of the School of Journalism, who told them that they valued their principles too highly. Next they called upon Smith, who said, "We're living under a dictatorship and the best thing to do is to submit to those in authority," adding that he would "dismiss the entire faculty and 4,000 students before offending the Louisiana Senator."

Most LSU students sympathized with the editors but, fearing loss of their state jobs, few supported them. The Southern Student Editors Board, however, adopted a resolution condemning censorship at LSU and praising the journalism students. Long warned that he would order the expulsion of additional students if they criticized him. "I like students," the Kingfish said, "but this state is putting up the money for that college, and I ain't paying anybody to criticize me." Ultimately 22 of the petitioners and 4 staff members apologized to Long and were readmitted. Seven students refused and were permanently barred. LSU alumni created a fund that enabled them to enroll at the University of Missouri, from which they graduated.

The episode demonstrated the limits on political dissent within the Kingfish's kingdom. The Southern Association of Colleges and Secondary Schools began an investigation of the abuse of academic freedom at LSU in 1934, but it was not completed before Long's death, and then was terminated.

Huey's defenders claimed that his injection of money into the state university outweighed this politicization and abridgement of academic freedom. No such rationalization could justify his neglect of elementary and secondary education in Louisiana. Although state expenditures soared under Long and his successors, the state's contributions to public schools actually declined, teachers' salaries were reduced, and the gap between white and black schools widened. Unlike universities, the public schools did not field high-profile bands or football teams; consequently they were not a priority. Long boasted that he was eliminating illiteracy, yet the improvements in Louisiana were hardly dramatic, were accomplished chiefly with federal

and private money, and occurred more rapidly under his pred-
ecessors and his successors than under him.

In 1933, after four years of Long's rule, the United States
Bureau of Education report ranked Louisiana forty-fourth in
general education, forty-seventh in literacy, and forty-seventh
in attendance. That year unpaid salaries to teachers reached
$1.4 million. Already low when the Kingfish became governor,
salaries declined every year he was in office. The reductions
appear greater if one deducts the money paid in anti-Long New
Orleans from the figures used to compute a statewide average.
In 1932 black elementary teachers were paid but $219 per year,
white ones $622. The disparity between white and black teach-
ers' salaries was greater at the end of Long's term than at its
beginning. By 1935 the school year had declined to 156 days for
white schools and 100 days for black ones. The paltry appropriations for education did not fully reflect the decline, however,
because inflated procurement of supplies and construction of
buildings provided profits to political cronies.

Huey believed that an honorary degree might furnish academic credentials and, when Tulane rebuffed his overtures,
accepted one from Loyola, a private Jesuit university in New
Orleans, on February 2, 1931. Ostensibly, the degree was
awarded for editing and annotating a compilation of the constitutions of Louisiana, although his staff did the work on the
book.

When it came to attracting attention, no one could outdo
Long. He generated enormous publicity for himself and his
state, much of it negative, all of it entertaining. For three weeks
beginning on February 17, 1931, he participated in a mock
debate in the press over proper etiquette for eating cornpone
and potlikker, which provided comic relief to Americans frustrated by economic hardship. (Potlikker is the liquid remaining
in a pot after vegetables, sometimes seasoned by pork, are
boiled in water. Southerners eat it with cornpone, a crusty
bread made with cornmeal.) Relatively inexpensive, potlikker
was a staple for farmers and sharecroppers during the Great
Depression. Usually they crumbled the cornpone into the
soupy potlikker and scooped it up with a spoon. Long argued

that etiquette required that cornpone be dunked into potlikker rather than crumbled. Julian L. Harris, the news director of the Atlanta *Constitution,* wrote a satirical article contending that southern tradition mandated crumbling. Soon letters and comments poured into the *Constitution,* which ran daily articles on the controversy.

Other papers joined the crusade; a Paris nespaper reported the "potliqueur et cornpone" debate. "Amos 'n' Andy" discussed it on the radio and politicians chose sides. Governor William H. ("Alfalfa Bill") Murray of Oklahoma argued that cornpone should be "crumbled as food for human beings and dunked as food for hound dogs." Governor Doyle E. Carleton of Florida advocated dunking on scriptural grounds. "Down here most of us are Baptists and we maintain that dunking does not go deep enough," he wrote, adding that "the immersion must be an absolute and a complete submerging." Carleton quoted II Kings 4:41, in which the prophet Elisha called for meal and "cast it into the pot." Finally, the affair petered out, with a large majority favoring crumbling. Some thought the mock debate demeaning to Southerners, but Long claimed it had a serious side—potlikker was cheap and healthy and the debate encouraged people to eat it.

In August and September of 1931 Long engaged in a debate that reaped publicity but no tangible results. By the third year of the Depression the price of cotton, the principal crop of many southern states, had plummeted. Long believed the problem was overproduction, and urged a ban on the planting of cotton in 1932 to increase demand. He issued an invitation to Southern governors to meet August 21 in New Orleans and adopt a plan to prohibit the planting of cotton in 1932. A majority of those who attended endorsed the plan.

Long summoned a special session of the legislature that unanimously approved a "cotton holiday" for Louisiana farmers and Huey signed the bill dressed in a cotton nightshirt. But to succeed, every southern state would have to approve the holiday. The key state, Texas, produced more than one-fourth of the crop. Long exhorted Texas to support his proposal, but the governor and legislature adopted a law mandating reduction of cotton acreage instead of a total ban of planting. An enraged Long charged that legislators had been "bought like a sack of corn to vote against the cotton prohibition plan . . . they have paid them off like a slot machine." He claimed that special interests had bribed officials with "the blandishments of wine, women, and money." Texas State Representative T. H. McGregor responded by calling the Kingfish "an arrogant jackass who brays from Louisiana . . . an ignoramus, a buffoon, a meddler and a liar who has the impudence and arrogance to . . . dictate to the people of Texas." The Texas Senate overwhelmingly enacted a resolution claiming that Long's charge of bribery was "not only untrue but carries the vice of a lie and the venom of a liar . . . and its author is a consummate liar."

Long's proposal was hopelessly impractical. Unless Egypt, India, Brazil, and China banned planting, the ban in the United States would have been ineffective; moreover, although some farmers might survive a year without planting, sharecroppers and tenant farmers could not. The Kingfish's program was defeated by the South Carolina legislature and the governor of North Carolina refused to summon a special session to consider it. Ironically, as a U.S. Senator, Long voted against acreage reductions mandated by the Agricultural Adjustment Administration. And in 1932 Louisiana was the only state that increased rather than reduced cotton acreage.

The potlikker debate and cotton controversy brought Long no real power. In the Democratic gubernatorial primary of January 19, 1932, however, he demonstrated that although he remained a minnow in national circles, he was still Kingfish of Louisiana. The primary would select Huey's successor as governor and he wanted a puppet. He selected Oscar K. Allen, an old Winnfield friend who had been elected to the state Senate in 1928 and whom he had appointed to head the Highway Commission. Fournet was the candidate for lieutenant governor on the "Complete the Work" ticket.

Allen was a complete nonentity whose only qualification was slavish devotion to the Kingfish. One of Long's assistants, in recommending Allen, told Huey: "He'll do anything you want. Nobody else will. You can be in Washington and still run things down here." Some considered Allen, who was silver-haired, dignified and soft-spoken, to be dimwitted; he was in fact a successful businessman with at least average intelligence. Middle-aged in 1932, he lacked stamina and suffered from heart disease, although most people were unaware of his health problems.

Candidate Allen was completely overshadowed by his mentor. The electorate realized that in voting for Allen they were actually voting for Long; the primary thus became a referendum on Longism. Allen received better financing than his opponents and better organizational support than had been available to Huey. The Old Regulars, who by this time had made peace with Long, put the machine in New Orleans at Allen's disposal. Long's popularity in the country parishes and the backing of such local bosses as Leander Perez virtually ensured Allen's election.

Four other candidates entered the race, but Allen's only serious challengers were Cajun politician Dudley J. LeBlanc and wealthy New Orleans attorney George S. Guion. LeBlanc, a French Catholic, was a hearty campaigner and eloquent speaker, but had little appeal for the Protestants of north Louisiana. Guion was obscure and did not command a statewide following.

The election caused a schism in the Long family. Earl Long wanted to run for lieutenant governor and Allen wanted him on the ticket, but Huey refused, because Earl had a mind of his own and might even dominate the weak-willed governor. Earl decided to run on the Guion ticket, and the entire Long family backed him.

Despite the bitter campaign, few expected a close election. Earl called Huey the "yellowest physical coward that God had ever let live," and claimed that even Huey's wife Rose intended to vote for Guion. However, LeBlanc was the more formidable adversary and Huey directed most of his attention to attacking the Cajun. The conflict degenerated into racist hyperbole; Long attacked LeBlanc for operating a burial insurance society for blacks and LeBlanc retaliated by calling Long and Allen "nigger lovers." When LeBlanc proposed state old-age pensions, Long objected that blacks would receive them and that it would waste money. Neither Long nor LeBlanc had much genuine sympathy for blacks.

No one talked about Allen. Campaign literature featured Long's photograph rather than Allen's. LeBlanc attacked the Kingfish, announcing that he stood "for ridding this state of Long and all his blood-sucking, tax-eating, bribe-giving and bribe-taking crowd." By this time Long had come to believe that public support was fickle, manipulation of the election machinery more reliable. The Old Regulars delivered their vote, as did Perez. Machine politics produced a resounding victory for Allen, who polled 214,699 votes to 110,048 for LeBlanc and 53,756 for Guion. Jefferson, St. Bernard, and Plaquemines, the latter two parishes dominated by Perez, returned incredible majorities for Allen. St. Bernard, with 2,194 registered voters, reported 3,152 votes for Allen and each member of his ticket and none for any other candidate. In one precinct the voters were recorded voting in alphabetical order.

Allen's victory and the removal of the Cyr permitted Long to resign as governor and take his seat in the U.S. Senate. Huey announced that he would never again run for state office; his ambitions were national.

Arriving in Washington on January 24, 1932, Huey received reporters in his hotel room, dressed in silk pajamas. The following day he appeared on the floor in a loud suit and flouted Senate traditions. As he entered the chamber, Long ignored the rule against smoking and walked to the front puffing on a cigar. After taking the oath, he sauntered around slapping senators on the back and poking them in the ribs. The *New York Times* compared him to a frisky colt.

Huey was not impressed with his colleagues and the feeling was mutual. He observed that the Senate "was just like the Louisiana Legislature except it is . . . maybe a little better." He became homesick. Long had never lived outside Louisiana for long and his family, which did not accompany him to Washington, did not visit. Huey, who roomed at the Mayflower Hotel and frequented nightclubs, moved to the Broadmoor, where he shared a suite with his bodyguards, who served as cooks, valets, and companions. Huey did not enjoy parties and was seldom invited. Alice Lee Grosjean stayed in Louisiana and they rarely met. She remained a part of the administration, however, and became supervisor of public accounts. Long's secretary in Washington, Earle Christenberry, became a member of the inner circle and a key figure in the Share Our Wealth crusade.

"I had come to the United States Senate with only one project in mind," Huey wrote, "which was that . . . I might do something to spread the wealth of the land among all of the people." Long pursued this objective tenaciously. Uninterested in the mundane affairs of Congress, he used the Senate as a forum to express his views to a national audience. He did not sponsor a single important bill and no senator sought his endorsement to cosponsor a bill. The most votes one of his bills ever received was 20 at a time when the Senate had 96 members. His arrogance, crude behavior, and feuds with Democratic leaders made him a pariah. Pat Harrison of Mississippi commented in 1934 that "in my view the opinion of the Senator from Louisiana is less respected by the membership of this body as a whole and by the country than that of any other Senator here."

Long considered himself a progressive, but only Burton K. Wheeler of Montana expressed any affection for him, and even Wheeler believed Long's methods misguided. Huey's voting record was not notably progressive: He consistently supported high tariffs and enforcement of prohibition. On economic issues he was slightly left of center. More conspicuous by his absence than by his presence in the Seventy-second Congress, Long was absent for 81 and present for only 56 of the days remaining in the session.

Oratory was Long's principle reason for wanting to be in the Senate. He proved the most flamboyant critic of concentrated wealth in either house. In March Long delivered two lengthy tirades against maldistribution of wealth. On April 4 he made his most important speech, entitled the "Doom of America's Dream." Long concluded that modern mass production was oppressive and that America was doomed unless wealth were redistributed. "God Almighty has warned against this condition," he said, adding that Thomas Jefferson, Andrew Jackson, Daniel Webster, Theodore Roosevelt, and William Jennings Bryan had done likewise. On April 12, Huey proposed a 65 percent surtax on incomes greater than $2 million and a 65 percent levy on estates of more than $20 million. On April 27 he introduced an amendment to limit annual income to $5 million. "I'm advocating what the Lord gave Moses," Long insisted. "What is a man going to do with more than $1,000,000?"

Each Long proposal polled only a handful of votes. Senator Joseph Robinson considered Long's appeals sheer demagoguery: "It is easy to arouse class hatreds, but more difficult to find an adequate remedy." Long concluded his April 27 oration by demanding new leadership for the Democratic Party and resigned from his committees. Robinson, leader of the Democratic majority in his chamber, termed it "a comic opera gesture."

On May 12 Long rose on the Senate floor to attack President Herbert Hoover, financier Bernard H. Baruch, and Eugene Meyer, governor of the Federal Reserve Bank. His most venomous insults, however, were directed at Robinson. Long had the Senate clerk read a list of corporate clients of Robinson's law firm. "The Senator's law firm represents every nefarious interest on the living face of the globe," he said. Ironically, the first client on the list was Long's close friend, the magnate Harvey Couch. Robinson's defenders pointed out that the senator was not active in the partnership to which his name was attached and received no profits from its clients.

By late May both parties were looking toward their presidential nominating conventions. The Democrats were to convene June 27 in Chicago. As he had in 1928, Long bypassed the Louisiana tradition of selecting delegates at a convention and engineered the appointment of a delegation that he headed. His outraged opponents selected a rival delegation. Adding to the confusion, Long arranged a rump convention that pledged its support to a minor Louisiana politician.

Unimpressed with the Democratic candidates, Long first suggested that the Democrats nominate Senator George W.

Norris of Nebraska, a Republican. Asked how he felt about Franklin Roosevelt, Huey responded: "He ain't got a chance." Asked if he would accept the vice-presidential nomination, he snapped: "Huey Long ain't vice to anybody or anything."

Roosevelt courted Long's support and Huey changed his mind; he became convinced that the New York governor sympathized with the poor. In Atlanta Roosevelt said: "The millions who are in want will not stand by silently forever while the things to satisfy their needs are within easy reach." Then he wrote Long: "You and I are alike for the rights in behalf of the common man of this country." Norris clinched the argument in favor of Roosevelt when he suggested that he and the Kingfish announce their endorsement simultaneously.

Long pledged the entire Louisiana delegation to the New Yorker. The Long delegation survived challenges before the credentials committee, the full national committee, and on the floor. Huey eloquently defended his delegation. When a rival charged that Long's delegation did not represent the Democratic Party in Louisiana, Long thundered: "I am the Democratic Party in Louisiana!"

The seating of the Roosevelt supporters from Louisiana demonstrated that Roosevelt controlled a majority of delegates to the convention. However, party rules required a two-thirds majority for nomination and Roosevelt fell short on each of the first four ballots. Roosevelt's campaign manager, James A. Farley, asked Huey to help hold the Mississippi and Arkansas delegations and to attempt to persuade favorite-son candidates, such as Governor Bill Murray of Oklahoma, to withdraw in favor of the New Yorker. Huey arrived at Murray's suite before the Oklahoman had arisen, banged on the door, and demanded to know why a man who claimed to be a farmer slept so late. Then, while Murray shaved and Long urged him to support Roosevelt, he ate Murray's breakfast, which had been sent up by room service. Murray refused to withdraw but the Mississippians and Arkansans stuck with Roosevelt. On the fifth ballot House Speaker John Nance Garner of Texas released the California delegates pledged to him so they could vote for

Roosevelt. Others jumped aboard the Roosevelt bandwagon and he won a two-thirds vote. The next day Garner was nominated for vice-president.

Long's work for Roosevelt was effective and experience as a national power broker was exhilarating. He decided to campaign for Roosevelt to enhance his own reputation and to claim credit for a Democratic victory. The New Yorker, however, learned to be cautious in dealing with the egotistical Louisianan. Roosevelt realized that Long's own ambitions took precedence over the Kingfish's desire to help the party.

After the convention Long rushed back to Louisiana to take command. Increased expenditures and falling revenues had left the treasury empty and Huey proposed new taxes. With the support of the Old Regulars, he was able to enact a variety of additional taxes, but they were unpopular with the public. Despite heavy borrowing, taxes inexorably soared. By 1935 Louisiana's government was the most expensive in the nation per capita. The debt had risen from $14 million when Long became governor to $96 million in 1933, and Louisiana's poor credit rating made it increasingly difficult to sell bonds.

Interested in expanding his influence while keeping his machine strong in Louisiana, Huey turned to the neighboring state of Arkansas in August 1932 and decided to support the reelection of long-shot candidate Hattie Caraway to the United States Senate. Caraway had succeeded her husband, winning a special election to complete his term on the promise that she would retire when it expired. When she decided to run for a full term, few people took her seriously. No woman had ever won a full term in the Senate and Caraway, a meek, dowdy widow, seemed an unlikely pioneer. Five well-known men entered the race, including a former governor and an ex-senator.

Long liked Caraway, who sat next to him in the Senate and consistently voted for his bills to redistribute wealth. He believed he could demonstrate his appreciation, and his influence beyond Louisiana, by helping her win. It appeared a quixotic crusade, but Long's campaign captivated Arkansas farmers as it did rural Louisianans. Brandishing a Bible, attacking Wall Street, he covered 2,100 miles and delivered 39 speeches to more than 200,000 Arkansans in just seven days. He campaigned with sound trucks and advance men, overshadowing Caraway in the campaign just as he had Allen. Caraway won decisively, her margin so large that the runner-up declined to run in a second primary. Long had worked a miracle. He was no mere state figure. What he had done in Arkansas he might do in other states.

After his Arkansas campaign Long conducted another whirlwind campaign in Louisiana in the Democratic Senate primary of September, 1932, backing Congressman John H. Overton, a Longite, against the incumbent Broussard, who had become his bitter enemy. Once again, Long, rather than the candidate, dominated the campaign. The Old Regulars backed Overton and the Long machine controlled the election through flagrant use of dummy candidates: More irregularities occurred in the election of Overton than ever before. Overton won by a vote of 181,464 to 124,935. Having become virtually uncontested ruler of Louisiana, Long wanted to become Kingfish of the entire United States.

CHAPTER SIX

Share Our Wealth

❖
❖

James A. Farley knew that in offering to campaign for Roosevelt, Long was actually campaigning for himself. Farley, who wanted to avoid taking attention from Roosevelt, also feared that Long might lose votes. On the other hand, Huey had to be treated gingerly; Roosevelt wanted his support and knew the Kingfish's ego bruised easily.

In midsummer Huey unveiled a plan for the fall campaign: The Democratic party would provide him with a train to tour all the major states. Farley was appalled. He and Roosevelt decided to limit Long's campaign to states that the Democrats considered safe or hopeless. When Farley telephoned the Kingfish to inform him, Huey was furious. "I hate to tell you, Jim, but you're going to get licked," he said. "Hoover is going back into the White House . . . I tried to save you, but if you don't want to be saved, it's all right with me."

Roosevelt tried to pacify Long by inviting him to lunch at Hyde Park. The candidate had never met the Kingfish, although they had conversed by telephone. Huey arrived dressed in a loud suit, orchid shirt, and pink necktie. Roosevelt asked Long to sit at his right and they talked throughout the meal. When Huey got boisterous, Franklin's mother asked a fellow diner, "Who is that awful man sitting on my son's right?"

Long accepted his assignment with resignation, and campaigned energetically with funds from his Louisiana backers. Farley sent him to North Dakota, South Dakota, Nebraska, and

Kansas, rural states where Long could address farmers who responded to his earthy humor, biblical quotations, and promise to redistribute wealth. Huey remarked: "We would have lost North Dakota if I hadn't gone there and straightened things out. I have been in South Dakota and we will carry that state."

After Roosevelt defeated Hoover, the Kingfish claimed credit. Although Long exaggerated his role, Farley conceded that Huey was more effective than party leaders had anticipated. "We never again underrated him," Farley said. He added that if he had permitted Long to campaign in Pennsylvania, which the Democrats lost narrowly, they might have won.

Long looked forward to the lame-duck session of Congress. He thought he would be influential in the next administration and decided to assert himself in the remaining months of Hoover's term. *Time* featured Huey's picture on the cover and predicted that he would be the most influential Southern Democrat in the Roosevelt administration.

Nevertheless, the Long-Roosevelt relationship was turbulent. Huey visited the president-elect at his cottage in Warm Springs, Georgia, and found the New Yorker genial but evasive. "When I talk to him he says 'Fine! Fine! Fine!'" the Kingfish complained. "But Joe Robinson goes to see him the next day and again he says 'Fine! Fine! Fine!' Maybe he says 'Fine!' to everybody." Long had never met a person as suave as the incoming president and it is unlikely that Roosevelt had ever encountered anyone like the Kingfish. Their competing ambitions became a recipe for conflict.

On opening day of the congressional session Long rose to condemn a Hoover proposal and digressed to lecture the incoming president. Roosevelt, he proclaimed, had been elected so "that he might carry out the one great fundamental necessary principle of the decentralization of wealth." The president-elect should dismiss the party leaders in Congress and select new ones, he suggested.

Long remained otherwise quiet during December, but in January he staged a filibuster against the banking bill of Senator Carter Glass because it favored national banks at the expense of state ones. While Long temporarily paralyzed the Senate, Will

Rogers wrote: "Imagine ninety-five Senators trying to outtalk Huey Long. They can't get him warmed up." The Senate passed the Glass bill but the House defeated it.

During Long's filibuster Roosevelt went to Washington to consult with Hoover. The Kingfish demanded an appointment with the president-elect to discuss his plans for limiting wealth: "I'm going to ask him 'Did you mean it, or didn't you mean it?'" Long emerged from the meeting pacified by Roosevelt's charm. "He is the same old Frank," Huey told reporters. "He is all wool and a yard wide." The Kingfish admitted Roosevelt knew more about the Bible than he did. Asked if the incoming president wanted to crack down on him for defying the Democratic leadership, Long replied, "He don't want to crack down on me. He told me, 'Huey, you're going to do just as I tell you,' and that is just what I'm a-going to do."

Huey demonstrated less respect for his colleagues in the Senate. "A mob is coming to hang the other ninety-five of you damned scoundrels," he told a fellow senator, "and I'm undecided whether to stick here with you or go out and lead them." The hostility was mutual. Wheeler observed that "Pat Harrison hated Huey like no one was hated in the Senate in my time." Glass referred to Long privately as "the creature who seems to have bought and stolen his way into the United States Senate," and Harry Byrd of Virginia asked to be assigned a different seat on the floor so he would not remain next to Long "even if I have to sit on the Republican side."

Two weeks after Roosevelt's inaugural on March 4, Long introduced three bills to redistribute wealth. One imposed a capital levy on fortunes, beginning at 1 percent on $1 million and doubling on each additional million; a second limited yearly income to $1 million; and the third restricted individual inheritances to $5 million. On March 17, Long delivered a lengthy speech implying that Roosevelt supported his bills. They were assigned to the Judiciary Committee and died there. On May 12, Long moved to amend revenue legislation by adding his capital levy plus limitations on incomes and inheritances. When Wheeler asked Huey how he intended to redistribute the money obtained from his taxes, Long conceded that he had not developed a plan for redistribution. He withdrew the capital levy to obtain support for the taxes, yet both were defeated 50–14. Long, angry at losing by such a margin, charged that the banker J. P. Morgan had bribed the Roosevelt administration to oppose his measures.

An incident on August 26, 1933, at the Sands Point Country Club on Long Island further damaged Huey's image. Attending a ball and dinner at the invitation of composer Gene Buck, Long got drunk, flirted with women, and insulted waiters. He called a black musician "coon" and "shine" and seized a dinner plate from a plump woman, declaring: "You're too fat already. I'll eat this." Long left for an hour to table-hop, and returned holding a napkin to a bleeding eye. He had attempted to urinate between the legs of a man in front of him in the men's room and when Long missed his target, the man punched him.

Long's attempts to explain the incident added to his humiliation. At his next public appearance he ordered his bodyguards to beat journalists who attempted to photograph his bandaged eye. Returning to Louisiana, he issued conflicting statements. "A member of the house of Morgan slipped up behind me and hit me with a blackjack," he told one reporter. Later he said five Wall Street agents had cut him with a knife. The management of the country club replied: "Senator Long's statement about being ganged is, of course, not worthy of comment."

A theme park manager offered Huey $1,000 to appear in a Coney Island freak show. A *Collier's* editor suggested awarding a gold medal to Long's assailant and used $1,000 mailed in by readers to mint a medal featuring a Kingfish with a black eye, wearing boxing gloves, reclining in a washstand.

Long contributed to the farce by writing a letter to Al Capone in a federal penitentiary. If he would claim credit for punching the Kingfish, Long suggested, the Democratic leadership, prompted by their millionaire supporters, would arrange his pardon. "Becoming thus honored and aligned with Morgan & Co., the government has to release you from jail and pay you back whatever you paid on income taxes," Huey wrote. "Instead of being classed with small fry criminals, you will stand with the crew that has starved and killed by the millions." Long wrote satirically, although reporters, and some biographers, took it literally. *Literary Digest* predicted that the affair would destroy Long politically but miscalculated the value of even unfavorable publicity to the Kingfish. There was still a mule's stubbornness—and a mule's kick—in Long.

Shortly after taking his seat in the Senate Long decided that it was time to write an autobiography; otherwise, fate might deny him a place in history. Too restless and impatient to write the book himself, he dictated it to his secretary and hired a New York journalist to edit it. After publishers rejected the manuscript, which provided few insights into his life, Huey incorporated his own company. Long printed 50,000 copies of *Every Man a King*, sold about 20,000 for $1 each, and gave away the rest. When he encountered Will Rogers, Long told him about the book and the humorist said he had also written one that failed to sell. "I'm smarter than you," Long replied. "I'm going to give mine away." Huey sold the book cheaply because he was more interested in obtaining publicity than money.

On February 23, 1934, Long incorporated a Share Our Wealth Society and copyrighted the terms "Share Our Wealth" and "Share the Wealth." He conceived the organization late one night and dictated his thoughts to Christenberry, but the idea had germinated since his 1918 letter to the New Orleans *Item* about the evils of concentrated wealth. Long, who initially emphasized taxation, not redistribution, now created an infrastructure to accomplish his program.

The Share Our Wealth Society had local affiliates nationwide. Anyone wanting to form a club merely wrote to Long, designated himself as president, and provided a list of members' names and addresses. Long compiled a massive mailing list to which he sent his autobiography, Senate speeches, pamphlets, tracts, and an instructional manual, all mailed under the franking privilege. Each member received a card reading: "Share Our Wealth Society—Every Man a King."

The clubs charged no dues but accepted donations. Ranging from 10 to 200 members, the clubs met in homes, churches, public auditoria, and lodge halls. Members subscribed to the

American Progress, read articles about sharing wealth, and discussed methods of implementing the Long Plan. Their chief task was to recruit members. The members staged parades and held rallies to proclaim the wisdom of wealth-sharing. Those who signed up believed they would be first in line to receive the wealth. The poor had little to lose by joining.

The society grew rapidly: It boasted 200,000 members within a month and within three months was adding 20,000 members daily. By the end of 1934 there were 3 million members; by the spring of 1935 there were 7.5 million. "It stood alone in one day, talked in two days, and began to run in three days. And now it is crying all over the length and breadth of the United States in one year," Long boasted on the society's first anniversary.

The most members were in Louisiana, Arkansas, Mississippi, and the other southern states. There were clubs throughout the Midwest and tens of thousands joined in New York and California. By mid-1934 Long was receiving more mail than all other senators combined, more even than the president. The mail to the Senate was delivered in two trucks: one for Huey, the other for all other senators. Long expanded his suite in the Senate Office Building to five rooms and had 25 assistants to open and classify mail. When workers became overwhelmed Long hired a night shift.

Huey told club leaders not to waste time on people who considered his plan impractical. "To hell with the ridicule of the wise street-corner politician," he wrote. "Will we allow the political sports, the high heelers, the wiseacres, and those who ridicule us in our misery and poverty, to keep us from organizing these societies in every hamlet so that they may bring back to life this law and custom of God and of this country?" Long's national organizer, Gerald L. K. Smith, told followers not to "let those white-livered skunks laugh at you."

The growth of the society was due largely to Smith, a Disciples of Christ minister hired to solicit members. Born in Wisconsin, educated at Valparaiso University, Smith preached at churches in Wisconsin, Illinois, and Indiana before becoming minister of the Kings Highway Christian Church in Shreveport a few months before the stock market crash of 1929. In 1932, when some members of his congregation were threatened with foreclosure on their homes, Long, at Smith's request, saved them and earned a disciple. Smith's friendship with Huey displeased his wealthy congregants and he resigned in 1934 before they could fire him. After a brief association with William Dudley Pelley's paramilitary Silver Shirts, he quit to accept a position from Long. A virulent anti-Semite, Smith became one of the more infamous hatemongers in America in the late 1930s, publishing a monthly, *The Cross and the Flag*, running unsuccessfully for the presidency and the U.S. Senate, and in the 1960s constructing a seven-story statue of Jesus and staging a Passion Play in the Ozark hamlet of Eureka Springs, Arkansas.

Blond, muscular, and charismatic, Smith was a more stirring speaker than Long. Submissive to Long, he nonetheless nourished a dark desire for power, an enormous ego, and a mastery of popular psychology. Long was one of the few personalities who could tame Smith, who came to consider himself an equal, perhaps even a rival. "He's needling me," Huey said of Smith. "You see that brown tie, suit—he got them from me. He wants to be like me."

Smith basked in Long's reflected glory, insisting that he and Huey were inseparable. "I've slept with him, eaten with him, talked with him, prayed with him and I know he is a man of God," Smith said. "All we need is 20,000,000 ballots." Long feared Smith's ambition and knew of his anti-Semitism, yet the Kingfish also knew that a minister would add to the credibility of the movement. Smith's oratory was attractive to rural fundamentalists. A master of pseudo-religious generalities, he implored audiences to "share, share, share," and to "pull down these huge piles of gold until there shall be a real job, not a little old sow-belly, black-eyed pea job but a real spending money, beefsteak and gravy, Chevrolet, Ford in the garage, new suit, Thomas Jefferson, Jesus Christ, red, white and blue job for every man."

Smith explained, "In order to succeed a mass movement must be superficial for quick appeal, fundamental for permanence, dogmatic for certainty, and practical for workability."

Smith believed that Share Our Wealth was a noble cause, although Long himself considered it simply a means to power. Still, Smith was pragmatic in his hero worship. "No great movement has ever succeeded unless it deified some one man," he explained. "The Share Our Wealth movement consciously deified Huey Long."

Smith began to organize Louisiana, then expanded to the rest of the South and by 1935 was speaking nationwide. He possessed broader vision and more voracious ambitions than other Longites. He hated Roosevelt intensely. "We're going to get that cripple out of the White House," Smith vowed. He claimed that Wall Street would stop at nothing to silence him. Once, a firecracker exploded while he was speaking. "They've tried to shoot me before," Smith shouted. "But if they ever did and I went down in a pool of blood there would be a thousand men in this parish to rise up in my place."

The Share Our Wealth Society attracted millions because it promised more than the New Deal. By confiscating annual income above $1 million and wealth in excess of $5 million, Long would provide each family with a home, a car, and a radio worth at least $5,000 ($50,000 in 1990 dollars) and an annual income of at least $2,500. He would also give old-age pensions to persons 60 or older, a bonus to veterans, and cut labor to a 30-hour week and an 11-month year. He would launch a war on disease, insanity, and drug addiction directed by the Mayo brothers. Long promised free college educations to students who passed entrance exams; others would attend vocational schools. He planned 1,000 new colleges employing 100,000 professors. Long would eliminate agricultural overproduction by limiting acreage, storing surpluses, and employing farmers on public works such as highways, golf courses, parks, buildings, and dams. Farmers would elect the secretary of agriculture. In place of the Federal Reserve System each state would elect one representative to a 48-member national bank modeled upon the plan of Father Charles E. Coughlin. Finally, Long would pardon those arrested for stealing food, and his plan would reduce incentives for crime; he would guarantee a job to every American.

"There is no rule so sure as the one that the same mill that grinds out fortunes above a certain size at the top, grinds out paupers at the bottom," Huey wrote. He considered the economic resources of the nation finite; only by taking from the poor did the rich become rich; only by taking from the rich could the poor escape poverty. "The whole thing is a seesaw," he wrote. "When one set of our people go high up in the air, the common people must come way down." Long encouraged hatred of the wealthy by charging: "Their fortunes came from manipulated finance, control of government, rigging of markets, the spider webs that have grabbed all businesses; they grab the fruits of the land, the conveniences and the luxuries that are intended for 125 million people, and run their heelers to our meetings to set up the cry, 'We earned it honestly.' The Lord says they did no such thing."

Huey claimed that authorities from Plato to the pilgrims supported redistribution of wealth. "It's all in Plato," he said. "I hadn't read Plato before I wrote my material on the Share the Wealth movement, and when I did read Plato afterwards, I found I had said almost exactly the same things. I felt as if I had written Plato's *Republic* myself." Huey also said that he planned to implement "the exact provisions of the contract of the Pilgrim Fathers in the year 1620 . . . that they should have an equal division of the wealth every seven years." Pope Pius XI and Theodore Roosevelt had advocated similar programs, he added.

Long said God was the source of his inspiration. "Herbert Hoover is calling together boards and commissions to find out what to do about it," he wrote in 1932. "The only dad-blamed thing on the living face of the earth that he needs to do is read his Bible." He claimed his wealth-sharing program was spelled out in the Book of Leviticus. "It tells you in there how to avoid depressions, how to keep everybody fed, and keep wealth turning over," he explained. "It even prophesies Al Capone and his gang in those Scriptures." Huey claimed that "not one historical fact that the Bible has ever contained has ever been disproved by any scientific discovery or by reason." He concluded, "Too many men running things think they're smarter than the Lord."

Long was alternately bellicose and gentle. "We had better redistribute wealth in America, by peaceful means while we can, or else it will be done through blood," he warned. As a child he had witnessed one of his cousins purchasing a mortgaged farm. "I thought that was the meanest thing I ever saw in my life, for my cousin to buy that poor man's farm when he didn't need it. 'Something awful's going to happen to him,' I thought. And sure enough, his wife died soon after that, and all sorts of misfortunes overtook him."

Long used statistical evidence as well. However, his statistics were outdated and perhaps inaccurate even when released. He did no economic research, but borrowed from others, sometimes without understanding. As his crusade grew, his statistics became more alarming. Initially he took statistics from the Industrial Relations Commission study of 1916 that concluded that 2 percent of the population owned 60 percent of the wealth, although he increased the percentage controlled by the upper 2 percent without additional research, assuming that the rich had increased their share since 1916. "There is no middle class," he complained. "Lords at the top; masses at the bottom." In 1935, without defining poverty, he claimed that 96 percent of all Americans lived in poverty. Also, he charged that 4 percent of Americans owned 87 percent of the wealth. Its simplicity enhanced the program's appeal; Huey emphasized the bounty instead of where the money would come from. "I could spend all night on details," he said in a radio address, "but I refuse to concede that people who listen to me are so devoid of common sense that they would believe that if we have things in abundance, there is any real trouble in handing them over to the people needing them." Most accounts have concluded that Long's plan constituted a radical redesign of capitalism and placed him on the left. Focusing on the confiscation of millionaire incomes and fortunes, they have neglected one of the more appealing aspects of Long's program to his contemporaries: No one but millionaires would pay any taxes! One could earn $999,999 (equivalent to $9.9 million in 1990 dollars), without paying one cent in taxes. In 1933 there were only 43 millionaires in the nation, the only ones who would be taxed under

Long's plan. Long recognized that there were conservative, even reactionary, aspects to his plan. "Other politicians had promised to re-make America; I had promised to sustain it," he wrote. Believing that most people were dissatisfied with their economic status yet feared change, he promised to correct social evils while he preserved the capitalist system.

The far left opposed the Long Plan more rigorously than the far right. Socialists and Communists denounced his scheme. "This plan is the only defense this country's got against Communism," Huey wrote. He opposed government ownership: "The government's messing around in business too much as it is." Long saw no difference between socialism and communism. He pointed out that there were only 80 members of the Communist Party in Louisiana. "They say that Huey P. Long is the greatest enemy that the Communists and Socialists have to deal with," he said.

Norman Thomas, a leader of the American Socialist Party, called Huey a fascist and predicted that if fascism came to America it would come in the guise of anti-fascism. In 1934 Thomas, debating Long, accused him of aspiring to become a dictator. "It was just that sort of talk, Senator Long," Thomas said, "that Hitler fed the Germans." Alexander Bittelman, a Communist journalist, was more direct. "Long says he wants to do away with concentration of wealth without doing away with capitalism," he wrote. "This is humbug. This is fascist demagogy."

The Kingfish faced more formidable rivals once the New Deal failed to eliminate unemployment. A host of messiahs attracted millions of followers; collectively, they represented a challenge to the established order and to Roosevelt's presidency. If the dissenters had joined forces, they might have overthrown the New Deal, although their leaders were jealously independent, their organizations fragmented, and their followers fickle. A hot meal might turn them into Democrats.

Father Charles E. Coughlin boasted the second-largest following after Long's. Born and educated in Canada, assigned a small parish in Royal Oak, a suburb of Detroit, he began broadcasting sermons in 1926 and, because he was a brilliant speaker, attracted a radio audience of millions. Coughlin became a critic of Hoover, then of Roosevelt, and advocated inflation by a silver-backed currency; he denounced international bankers for creating depressions. Supported by his bishop, he became increasingly strident and anti-Semitic as the depression deepened. Eventually, when he became virulently anti-Semitic, his superiors silenced him. Nonetheless, in 1934 and 1935 journalists observed similarities in the programs of Long and Coughlin and pointed out that their followings overlapped.

Some followers admired both, but the leaders did not get along. Enormously egotistical, Coughlin was no more willing to take orders from Long than the Kingfish was from Coughlin. Huey was contemptuous of Coughlin's political skills and the priest called the Long Plan "unthinkable radicalism." "*Social Justice* refuses to accept the theory of confiscating the wealth in the nation and then, afterwards, dividing it equally among its citizens," Coughlin wrote. "Some citizens labor more assiduously than others. Some labor more intelligently than others. To these is rightfully attributed a greater share of wealth than to the mental sluggards and to the indolent." Potential allies, Long and Coughlin could unite only if they disliked Roosevelt more than they disliked each other.

Francis E. Townsend, another critic of the New Deal, claimed a following that rivaled Long's and Coughlin's. An elderly, frail physician, Townsend appealed to the aged with his proposal to pay retirees a monthly pension of $200, financing it with a sales tax. Those over 60 would have to retire from work and spend each stipend before next month's check arrived, a system designed to provide security for old people and pump money into the economy. Unlike Long and Coughlin, Townsend was not a riveting speaker or a charismatic personality, although he commanded millions of followers. Townsend considered an alliance with Coughlin and praised Long editorially. "The vast majority of the American public agree with Huey that incomes should be limited," he wrote. The United Press reported, "Both Long and Townsend admit that their strength overlaps. Hundreds, perhaps thousands, of persons in California belong to both the Townsend club and the

Share the Wealth club." A paper in upstate New York supported a 1936 ticket comprised of Long for president, Townsend for vice president, and Coughlin for "treasurer."

Townsend's fellow Californian, novelist Upton Sinclair, proposed a panacea called End Poverty in California (EPIC) and ran for governor advocating state-run factories where the unemployed could make their own necessities. Sinclair's following overlapped Townsend's, although the novelist labeled the Long Plan "not a plan at all, but merely a conglomeration of appealing political bait, a high income tax, and one or two steps toward limitation of accumulation of wealth. In no instance does it reach the real source of trouble, the private ownership of natural resources and production facilities operated for private profit."

Angry farmers filled the Midwest. "The middle and western states are crawling with radical farm leaders whose individual influence may be small and localized but whose aggregate power to make or break administrations would be great, if they are ever brought together in a national campaign," journalist Jay Franklin Carter wrote. Also, Governor Floyd Olson of Minnesota warned that Roosevelt would have to revive the economy if he hoped to avoid a third-party challenge in 1936. Olson implied that he would be willing to collaborate in such a movement.

Brothers Robert and Philip La Follette of Wisconsin also appeared ready to jettison the New Deal. Robert, as a U.S. Senator, and Phil, as governor, emerged as two successful insurgents. In 1934 they reincarnated the Progressive Party and swept the fall elections in Wisconsin. Appearing open to overtures from Long and Coughlin, their journal stated: "The *Progressive* may not agree with every conclusion reached by Father Coughlin and Senator Long. When they contend, however, as they have, that the tremendous wealth of this country should be more equitably shared for a more abundant life for the masses of people, we agree heartily with them."

The Corn Belt seethed with discontent, especially Iowa, where Milo Reno, leader of the Farm Holiday Association, led thousands of militant farmers. In 1932 he advocated a farm strike but it failed to spread beyond Iowa. In 1934, at 68, Reno knew his health was failing and sought allies who could help perpetuate his movement. He invited Coughlin, Olson, and Long to address his state convention in Des Moines; all three accepted, but Coughlin and Olson later withdrew.

The messiahs each viewed events from a particular perspective. Although all questioned the efficacy of the New Deal, each believed his own solution the most effective. The insurgent movement possessed a life of its own beyond any single leader. Dissent was broad yet shallow, and the desperate chose among the various schemes like hungry shoppers in a cafeteria selecting the most appealing dishes.

Although the programs offered by the dissident leaders were impractical, they identified genuine defects in the economy. Maldistribution of wealth was one cause of the Depression, as Long asserted; the elderly needed pensions, as Townsend pointed out; inflation could help debtors, as Coughlin perceived; overproduction led to low farm prices, as Olson and Reno knew; and economic planning was necessary, as Sinclair recognized. Before the 1936 presidential election, Roosevelt dealt with each facet of the problem and robbed the dissident leaders of their constituencies.

Long directed public attention to the inequitable distribution of wealth. His contribution was not to identify the problem but to publicize it. Simple, folksy speeches reduced economics to the language of the common man; few critics were as eloquent or as forceful. Of all the messiahs of the depression era he was the most successful politician, hence he posed the greatest threat to the New Deal.

Share Our Wealth was too good to be true. There were fewer millionaires in the United States than Long thought, and their fortunes were inadequate to provide the benefits he promised. There was no way to divide assets such as railroads or factories. If they were taken from their owners, there would be no expertise to run them. Long claimed his confiscation of millionaire assets would reap $170 billion, yet the value of all assets in private hands was only $70 billion to $90 billion in 1933. The confiscation of the liquidatable assets of millionaires would provide only $1.50 for each family that earned less than $2,500 annually.

Every reputable economist who examined the Long Plan ridiculed it. To begin with, a survey of the assets of every family in the United States would be taken by distributing questionnaires to each household. Millionaires would be "on their honor" to report their assets, requiring an army of auditors and police state regimentation to prevent cheating.

Long apparently assumed that everyone who possessed wealth gained it at the expense of others. When Huey asked Roosevelt to support his plan, the president responded by asking, "Can you suggest an equitable way of segregating great fortunes owned in this country and gained through the abuse of social ethics from those which were gleaned by ingenuity or as compensation for honest toil plus good management?"

There were additional flaws. For example, Long talked in terms of families, yet made no provisions for families of different sizes or unmarried, widowed, or divorced persons. His plan to confiscate estates and other nonliquidatable properties was a one-time event; after that there would be nothing to redistribute in future years. It was highly questionable to assume that individuals would continue to earn high incomes and accumulate property, only to see it taken by the government. There would have been no incentives for people to continue to accumulate wealth, and if they did not, there would be nothing to tax after the initial confiscation. Senator Alben Barkley of Kentucky correctly termed the Long Plan a "visionary hallucination."

Farm leaders pointed out that only nonperishable products could be stored in warehouses, as Long advocated, and such products constituted only a fraction of total production. Huey's scheme to use farmers on public works projects was naïve, because many of them lacked the skills to build dams, bridges, or buildings; furthermore, they could not abandon homes and families to work in areas where construction was needed. American industry required constant infusions of capital and if Long taxed away such capital there would be no expansion, and money would not be available to repair or replace machinery and buildings. The Kingfish seemed to envision a static economy. His belief that one could help the poor only by taking from the rich was simplistic.

Arguments about the practicality of Long's plan are largely academic, because Congress would never pass it and it violated the provision in the Fourteenth Amendment, that "No person shall be deprived of life, liberty, or property without due process of law." Huey's sincerity in advocating it is dubious. When an associate told him that Share Our Wealth was unworkable, he conceded it, and added, "When they figure that out, I'll have something new for them." Long told another supporter that sharing the wealth was merely a scheme to attract votes and he had no intention of implementing it. However, he added, "there are twenty million votes in that." Harley Bozeman said, "Huey wasn't sincere about Share Our Wealth. He didn't intend to 'deal' it until FDR with his appeal made him."

Critics observed that Long did not practice in Louisiana what he preached in Washington. They suggested Long never helped anyone unless there was something in it for him. "Lust for power, not compassion for the poor, is his driving impulse," *Collier's* concluded.

In a similar vein, Thomas asked; "If Mr. Long is in earnest, how could he tolerate conditions in the cotton country where people are evicted and driven from their homes without his lifting a hand?" Others pointed out that Long had blocked the Louisiana legislature's ratification of a constitutional amendment that would have limited child labor with the comment, "picking cotton is fun for the kids, anyway." Louisiana also refused to pay the prevailing wage on public works projects; when union leaders complained, Long told them they should be happy to get work at any wage. Neither did Louisiana have a minimum-wage law, old-age pensions, or unemployment compensation. Long advocated steeply graduated income taxes, yet Louisiana had no income tax until 1934, and then it was almost a flat rate. Louisiana did not create a Department of Public Welfare until after Long's death.

Although the Long Plan made no economic sense, it made a great deal of political sense. The Kingfish's advocacy of wealth sharing made him a formidable rival to Roosevelt. However, he raised expectations so high that disillusionment was inevitable. If he failed to produce results, he would ruin his credibility. Moreover, the plan could not withstand scrutiny by the national press in a presidential campaign.

Long's Share Our Wealth program appealed to blacks because they were the most abjectly poor. Black leaders in Louisiana told journalist Paul Hutchinson that if enfranchised, 90 percent of their people would vote for the Kingfish. Posing as an enemy of the rich, Huey delighted rural blacks by ridiculing plutocrats and attacking corporations. When his ambitions reached national proportions he began to court black voters. Smith instructed Share Our Wealth club leaders to "see that the colored man" registered, paying the poll tax so he could vote, because it was "our intention to get the vote of the colored man in the general election, when the Senator will run for President."

Still, Huey's championing of economic rights for blacks was entirely self-serving because he never expressed support for their political rights. In addition, those wanting to join the Share Our Wealth Society received mixed signals. A few northern chapters were integrated but the vast majority were segregated, and some blacks were refused membership cards. In the South, blacks were permitted to attend rallies as long as they remained around the edges of the crowd and did not mingle with whites. When two blacks attempted to attend a New Orleans meeting of ministers who supported wealth-sharing, the elevator operator shut the door in their faces, saying, "You were not invited."

The case for Huey Long as an active friend of black Louisianans was little stronger than the case for him as an active enemy. His claim to enlightenment rests on his refusal to resort frequently to virulent race-baiting, although he made some racist statements. Long was a typical Louisiana politician in his infrequent appeals to racism in the 1920s and 1930s. None of the Kingfish's opponents made race a major issue in any campaign in which Huey participated, and the myth of the "Lost Cause" did not dominate state politics as it had in the 1890s. The decline of the issue paralleled the reduction of blacks to political impotence. Blacks, who were 45.5 percent of registered voters in 1896, made up only 4 percent by 1900 and in 1906 Louisiana adopted the white primary, which excluded the few black voters from Democratic primaries. By 1906 only 1,342 blacks were registered (1.4 percent) although blacks constituted 47 percent of the population.

Long, a pragmatist, attacked more credible scapegoats such as millionaires and corporations, and he did not encourage black voting. When he ran for governor in 1924 there were 322,600 white voters registered and 955 black ones, only 0.3 percent of the total. When he was elected in 1928 the number of white voters had climbed to 377,246, blacks to 2,054, constituting 0.5 percent. By 1936, the year after Huey's death, white registration had risen to 641,609 and black registration had declined to 2,043, representing 0.3 percent, the same as in 1924. Whatever the potential economic benefits of the Long machine, it did not increase black participation in politics.

Long's personal views toward blacks were a mixture of contempt and paternalism. He believed blacks biologically inferior and incapable of succeeding economically on their own. The Kingfish was repelled by those he believed tainted with black blood. In 1932 he planned to include the registrar of the state land office, Lucille May Grace, on his state ticket but retracted his promise to her after one of her rivals spread a rumor that her ancestors included blacks. The Kingfish restored Grace to the ticket only after she hired two genealogists to reconstruct her family tree, and to prove it entirely Caucasian.

Long denounced the *Times-Picayune* as a newspaper "which claims to be a paper for white supremacy, but one of the leading executives of which is part Negro." He nicknamed Alvin Howard, a part owner of the daily, "Kinky," because of his curly hair and referred to a dark-complexioned *Picayune* executive as Leonard "Liverwurst" Nicholson. Huey used the term "nigger" in conversation and in writing circulars, but his printers changed the word to "Negro," and he condemned a political opponent, Shreveport businessman Andrew Querbes, for operating a "nigger" saloon and "dive."

As a struggling lawyer, Long refused a request to sue white

employers on behalf of blacks who were whipped and abused in a Winnfield lumber mill. "It is a matter which I cannot handle, although I don't doubt everything you say being true," he responded. "It would merely injure me and we would never get anything out of a suit." As governor, Long signed into law a 1928 bill that required racial segregation on passenger buses in Louisiana. Finally, as a senator, he refused to support legislation to outlaw lynching. "You can quote me as saying I'll vote 100 per cent against the Costigan-Wagner anti-lynching bill that's brought up there in Washington," he said. "We just lynch an occasional nigger." Asked about a 1935 lynching in Louisiana, he replied, "Anyway, that nigger was guilty."

Long wrote a pamphlet in 1934 to explain that his proposal to repeal the Louisiana poll tax would not permit blacks to vote. He argued: "An underhand and secret lie is being spread about that this amendment for free poll taxes will let the Negro vote in our elections. That is not true and everybody telling it either does not know the truth or doesn't want to know the truth. The free poll tax will not affect the status of the Negro at all. Negroes can pay and do pay their poll taxes now, but that doesn't give them any better chance to vote. It is the white primary that keeps the Negro out of our elections."

Long did nothing specific to help blacks in Louisiana and when it was feasible to discriminate against them, such as in education, he did so with a vengeance. In 1932 Louisiana schools spent $44.98 annually on each white student and only $7.88 on each black one. White libraries received $30,560.89 to only $818.20 for black libraries. The discrepancy was even greater in providing transportation to schools: Even though black schools were more isolated, the state spent $1,521,604.34 for 3,388 buses to transport white children and only $2,549.65 for 9 buses to convey blacks.

Moreover, Long's advisers included two of the more infamous racists of twentieth-century America, Smith and Leander H. Perez, who were beginning lengthy careers in race-baiting. Smith's pet hate was Jews, Perez's blacks, but Smith also hated blacks and Perez hated Jews. Long tolerated them because he did not care much about black rights and he needed

Smith's oratorical and organizing talents, and Perez's ability to deliver votes.

Long's attitude toward race was expedient; he never helped those who could not vote, and sacrificed the rights of minorities if it advanced his career. "My guess is that Huey Long is a hard, ambitious, practical politician," Roy Wilkins wrote after interviewing him. "He is far shrewder than he is given credit for. My further guess is that he wouldn't hesitate to throw Negroes to the wolves if it became necessary; neither would he hesitate to carry them along if the good they did him was greater than the harm."

Huey did not tolerate anyone, black or white, who thought for him- or herself. As he gazed at the White House, he knew that he would have to secure his base in Louisiana to challenge Roosevelt. An inveterate dissenter, he did not tolerate dissent within his own bailiwick; rather, he suppressed it ruthlessly.

CHAPTER SEVEN

Suppressing Dissent

❖
❖

Long's state provided a grim model for what he intended to do nationally. Instead of making Louisiana a "laboratory of democracy," as Robert M. La Follette did in Wisconsin, he made it a police state. In 1932, believing himself invulnerable in Louisiana, Huey assumed that his puppets would run the state under his orders. Unfortunately, rebellion threatened his national ambitions and his Louisiana machine, which careened out of control, requiring him to make frequent trips home. Initially defeated in a crisis in 1933, he counterattacked and by the end of 1934 was unchallenged. He destroyed local government and evoked chilling comparisons with Adolf Hitler.

Huey's alliance with the Old Regulars from 1930 to 1933 marked a change of direction. No longer an outsider, he became a boss who relied less on charisma and oratory than on regimentation. Now he was obsessed with power. John H. Overton's victory in Louisiana's Democratic senatorial primary in September 1932 had been won with the aid of the Old Regular machine, and he had not received strong support from the rural parishes that Long candidates usually commanded. Overton's election, however, rewarded a friend and punished a foe. Overton, a courtly, urbane lawyer, was one of the few Louisiana aristocrats who liked Long. Huey had supported his unsuccessful campaign for the U.S. Senate in 1918 and Overton had served as Long's attorney during the impeachment attempt of

1929. In 1931, with Huey's support, he had been elected to the U.S. House of Representatives.

While Overton grew in Long's esteem, U.S. Senator Edwin S. Broussard incurred his wrath. Broussard did not aid Huey when he was impeached and remained neutral when Long challenged Ransdell. In 1931 he termed Long "the worst governor Louisiana ever had," and the following year he opposed Long's "Complete the Work" ticket.

Overton defeated Broussard comfortably in the primary, yet played an insignificant role in his own campaign. The Kingfish told the candidate not to campaign because he was "as good as elected." Long delivered the speeches, raised the money, and selected Overton's campaign managers. The election was a referendum on Longism and Overton's credentials were irrelevant because everyone knew Long would control the vote. Long wanted to defeat Broussard so badly that he did not trust the democratic process. All his life he feared rejection and humiliation. "I'm always afraid of an election," he said. "You can't tell what will happen."

If Long's alliance with the Old Regulars guaranteed his candidates large majorities in New Orleans, it also ensured there would be no restraints on corrupt electioneering. Overton would have defeated Broussard in a fair vote, but the primary was thoroughly corrupt.

Long used hundreds of dummy candidates to secure favorable commissioners. In St. Landry Parish, District Judge Benjamin F. Pavy enjoined the commissioners obtained by use of dummies from serving, but they ignored the judge and participated anyway. When Pavy jailed them for contempt of court, Allen issued reprieves. Although Broussard was denied poll commissioners throughout Louisiana, in New Orleans the bias was insurmountable; he had 61 commissioners to 1,119 for Overton.

After his defeat Broussard filed charges of fraud with the Senate and demanded an investigation. The Senate Committee on Campaign Expenditures, chaired by Robert B. Howell of Nebraska, held hearings in New Orleans in October, 1932, and in February and November 1933. The October hearings were conducted by a subcommittee of Democrats Tom Connally of Texas and Samuel G. Bratton of New Mexico, who selected Samuel T. Ansell, former judge advocate general of the army, as committee counsel. Ansell, an imperturbable, aggressive attorney, detested Long, who served as Overton's attorney, and the two exchanged bitter recriminations. Long once threatened to take Ansell outside the federal building and beat him; Ansell replied that he would be happy to fight Huey without his bodyguards. Long called Ansell a "scoundrel, rascal, liar, thief, crook, and counterpart of Benedict Arnold." Ansell responded with two $500,000 libel suits, one still pending at Long's death.

The hearings produced hundreds of pages of embarrassing testimony about Huey's machine. "I do not know how they hold elections in Mexico or Russia, but I do not think they could surpass what has been going on in Louisiana since Huey P. Long was elected to the United States Senate," Earl Long testified.

Witnesses provided examples to support Earl's charges, such as the fact that St. Bernard Parish, with 2,500 registered voters, recorded 3,176 for Overton and 13 for Broussard. In one New Orleans precinct, tallies were recorded before the voting was completed; in another, voting began before the polls opened. Commissioners went to the homes of Overton supporters, permitted them to vote, then carried the ballots back and deposited them. A Broussard supporter who had lived in his precinct for 13 years was disqualified on the grounds that he did not meet the three-month residency requirement. In some precincts, new ballot boxes were substituted for the ones used for voting before the counting. Broussard commissioners were prevented from counting or witnessing the recording of votes. A commissioner testified that Broussard ballots were erased and marked for Overton. Several commissioners who refused to cheat for Overton were fired from city jobs. A man who said he could provide 30 votes for Overton was paid $400 by the State Highway Commission for a right-of-way on property he did not own.

Ansell hit a dead end when he traced Overton's financial trail to Seymour Weiss, who testified that he had paid bills with cash and kept no records. When Ansell asked why he did not keep records, Weiss responded: "Well, there are a couple of reasons. First, I did not want to, and second, it was too much trouble." When Ansell persisted by asking where Overton's money had been deposited, Weiss replied, "None of your business," and, encouraged by Long, gave the same answer to further questions. While Ansell pressed Weiss, Huey interjected, "Don't answer that question, on my instructions."

"On what ground?" Ansell asked.

"Because I said not to do so," Long replied.

"Is that sufficient?"

"That is plenty. Kingfish of the lodge."

Long's opponents expected the committee to cite him and Weiss for contempt of Congress, but the senators permitted them to evade questions without punishment.

The most sensational testimony focused on Huey's finances. Long correctly pointed out that this testimony was politically motivated because it did not pertain to the Overton election. However, it was no more political than Long's investigations of vice in New Orleans or his selective raids on gambling, designed explicitly to embarrass his enemies.

The most damaging witnesses were Huey's brothers, Julius and Earl, and he felt it was futile to refute them. "If I could lay bare to the world the exact amounts of graft taken from the funds of the various departments and institutions since my brother . . . became governor I am sure that it would be so astonishingly large that even I would be astounded," Julius testified. He claimed Huey had extorted $500 to $1,000 from every road contractor who did state business to finance his 1930 senatorial campaign, and added that his brother employed bodyguards to intimidate voters. "If anybody voiced opposition to Huey's candidates they were beaten up," Julius said.

Earl said Huey had been corrupt since his first race for public office, and described a meeting at which a representative of the New Orleans Public Service, Inc., had bribed the Kingfish. "He gave him one hundred $100 bills. I saw the bills. They were brand new. They looked like they had just come off a machine." Under cross-examination by Huey, Earl added:

"You told me that the man put the money in your bathrobe pocket. You told him that the ante wasn't strong enough and you thought he should have given a lot more than $10,000." Earl's charge undermined Huey's credibility because the Kingfish had based his career on opposition to organized wealth.

After Howell died in March 1933, Connally took control of the committee and reported to Congress in January 1934. Without recommending any course of action, Connally said frauds had been perpetrated, yet there was no evidence that Overton had participated. Although Broussard's charges were accurate, Connally concluded, Overton probably had received a majority of the vote that was cast honestly. The Senate referred the matter to a special committee, which dismissed the charges. By then Overton had been in his seat for more than a year-and-a-half and it would have taken a two-thirds vote of the Senate to expel him. His colleagues, who liked Overton better than Long, had no desire to expel him. The affair frustrated Connally. "I advise anyone who thinks he knows something about politics to go down in Louisiana and take a postgraduate course," he said. Huey replied, "Politics in Louisiana is as clean as an angel's ghost." He attributed the lengthy controversy to persecution, but added that he expected it: "I was born into politics, a wedded man, with a storm for my bride."

Long's Louisiana enemies continued to call for action. The hearings so angered Hilda Phelps Hammond that she created the Louisiana Women's Committee and petitioned Congress to expel Long and Overton. The women, mostly middle-class volunteers from New Orleans, auctioned family heirlooms to finance their work. Former Governor Parker still fought Long as well, telegraphing Vice President Garner: "Psychiatrists have said in my presence he is a dangerous paranoic. The Senate should have him permanently incarcerated in Washington. He is the greatest menace to American decency and civilization."

On June 20, 1933, Congressman Boliver Kemp died with about 18 months remaining on his term. Kemp had been neutral toward Long and the Kingfish had been unable to dominate his district. Long feared voters might elect an anti-Longite—most likely J. Y. Sanders, Jr.—to Congress. Although the state constitution mandated an election to choose a successor, Allen refused to call one for five months; Huey explained that an election would be too expensive. Voters demanded an election, filing lawsuits and petitions. Finally the district Democratic committee met secretly, without its anti-Long members, and certified Lallie Kemp, the congressman's widow, as the party nominee. On November 28, Allen, insisting there was too little time to hold a Democratic primary, scheduled a general election for December 5; only Kemp's name would be on the ballot. Outraged, Long's opponents obtained an injunction from a district judge prohibiting the distribution of ballots listing Kemp as the nominee, only to learn that the ballots had been printed and distributed before the committee met. Anti-Long leaders boycotted the election, three parishes within the district refused to appropriate money to pay for it, and local sheriffs swore in hundreds of special deputies to prevent delivery of ballots. One of the deputies, Hodding Carter, editor of the antiadministration Hammond *Courier*, lay in a ditch with a rifle, hoping he would not have to use it. On December 5, only 4,800 of the 45,000 registered voters cast ballots. In three of the nine parishes not a single vote was cast; in Slidell, the largest town, only 18 persons voted. On December 27, 19,500 voters participated in a "citizens" election, which Sanders won. Sanders and Kemp presented their credentials to Congress, which refused to seat either and ordered a new election, in which Sanders defeated Long's candidate, state Commissioner of Agriculture Harry D. Wilson, in April, 1934.

The Kingfish faced fiscal as well as political problems. Louisiana neared bankruptcy. Long pushed large tax increases through the legislature, and citizens responded with organized protests. In the fall of 1933 Huey began a statewide speaking tour to arouse support for his program, with disappointing results. Voters heckled him, condemned his war record and ridiculed the Sands Point incident; vandals tore down signs crediting the Long and Allen administrations with construction of highways and bridges. In November Long canceled his remaining speeches after being showered with eggs, stink bombs, and rotten vegetables in Alexandria.

Long's unhappy allies, the Old Regulars, sensed he was vulnerable. They had supported constitutional amendments to increase taxes in November 1932 and voters approved the rate increases, but the election had been fixed. In 16 precincts in New Orleans the vote on all 15 amendments was unanimous; in 15 others fewer than 10 votes had been recorded against any amendment. District Attorney Eugene Stanley convened a grand jury to investigate, but Long ordered Attorney General Gaston Porterie to supersede him and the jury returned no indictments. Stanley convened a second grand jury, yet Porterie replaced him again and dismissed the charges. Many New Orleanians, even those who collaborated with Long, found such tactics repulsive. Stanley convened a third grand jury, which indicted 512 election commissioners. Three were convicted but Allen pardoned them. Stanley had to drop charges against the others because the legislature passed a law requiring proof that errors in recording votes were deliberate.

The Louisiana Bar Association expelled Porterie for blocking Stanley's investigations and misdirecting grand juries. Long responded by creating a bar association whose officers were elected by the general public; it promptly elected Porterie president. The American Bar Association, however, refused to recognize Long's association.

New Orleans scheduled an election for city officials in January 1934, and Long demanded the right to name part of the ticket, excluding Stanley. Long met with Mayor Walmsley, who was seeking reelection. Although they could not agree upon a ticket, Walmsley thought he could win without Huey's help and hoped to obtain New Deal patronage if he broke with Long. Huey responded by entering his own ticket headed by John D. Klorer, father of the editor of the Louisiana *Progress*. On January 16, a week before the election, Old Regular officials found the state-appointed registrar of voters removing the names of their supporters from the voting rolls, despite a court order forbidding it. Stanley arrested the registrar and obtained an order placing the rolls in the custody of the sheriff. Long had Allen declare martial law and sent 400 National Guardsmen to New Orleans; city officials threatened to swear in 10,000 special deputies to fight the guard. Any incident could have provoked violence, but on election day, January 23, the voting was peaceful. Walmsley won 45 percent of the vote to 29 percent for Klorer, who did not choose to run in a second primary.

Walmsley's victory encouraged the Kingfish's opponents in the legislature to plan to remove Longite Speaker Allen Ellender and Governor Allen when the legislature convened in May. However, they fell three representatives short. Frustrated by their impotence, some said at a caucus on May 13 that they wanted to kill Long by storming his suite in the Heidelberg Hotel. They gave up because the Kingfish was protected by dozens of bodyguards, some armed with submachine guns.

When the legislature convened on May 14, Long counterattacked with benefits and threats that pummeled his enemies into submission. The benefits included laws exempting most homeowners from property taxes, a moratorium on small debts, abolition of the poll tax, and a reduction in the cost of automobile license plates. To compensate for lost revenue, taxes were placed on public utilities, the New Orleans Cotton Exchange, and daily newspapers with circulations of more than 20,000. The only newspapers that qualified were the New Orleans papers, which opposed Huey; he called it a "tax on lying." In 1936 the U.S. Supreme Court nullified the tax as an unconstitutional abridgement of freedom of the press, but for two years it constituted a weapon of reprisal in Huey's arsenal. Long also had the legislature halt the annual state appropriation of $700,000 for New Orleans street repairs.

Most of the legislation was intended to punish New Orleans. The legislature denied the city revenue by transferring authority to grant liquor licenses from municipalities to the state. Another act removed custody of ballot boxes from local sheriffs and gave it to state-appointed election supervisors. And to prevent Long's opponents from impounding boxes by court order, the legislature passed a bill providing that no court could impound records in the hands of a state official.

As the session progressed opposition melted away before

the Kingfish's onslaught; he grew increasingly arrogant and dropped the pretense of ruling through Allen. Long, a federal official, had no right to be present on the floor of the legislature, but dominated the proceedings. During the vote on the newspaper tax he personally cast the vote of an absent member. No one protested.

Long decided to overcome his defeat by Walmsley by re-electing two pro-Long congressmen from New Orleans in September. He supported incumbents Paul Maloney and Joe Fernandez against their Old Regular opponents and campaigned for Overton's brother, Supreme Court Justice Winston Overton, whom Thomas F. Porter challenged.

In July, Long, intending to discredit the Old Regulars, received legislative authorization to investigate gambling and prostitution in New Orleans. On July 17 Long announced that he would conduct the investigation himself, declaring, "The red light district has expanded to the point of national disgrace." Eight days later Allen declared martial law in New Orleans and dispatched 12 companies of the National Guard. Saying "the reign of vice is a thing of the past," Allen predicted that with vice eliminated the city would be "known as the center of learning and science; the gateway to all continents," and called upon ministers to suppress sin in the metropolis.

Walmsley called Long a composite of "Caligula, Nero, Attila, Henry VIII and Louis XI," and warned, "While some may drop in the defense of New Orleans, we will never surrender to this madman." He said Long, "a political degenerate, moral leper, coward and Al Capone," would "end up in an insane asylum."

Huey interrogated witnesses in the privacy of a hotel suite; no reporters, city officials, or defense attorneys were permitted, but the hearings were broadcast on radio. No one was surprised to hear about vice in New Orleans. Long said his investigation demonstrated that New Orleans was "the greatest cesspool of hell that has ever been known to the modern world." Nonetheless, there were no prosecutions.

The inquiry was a sideshow to the confrontation between the city and the state at the office of the registrar of voters. Just before midnight on July 30, Long sent 50 guardsmen to take possession of the office without declaring martial law until the troops had arrived. Walmsley obtained an injunction against the occupation but state officials ignored it; then the mayor swore in 400 special deputies and deployed them around the building. Long sent 600 additional guardsmen and for days the heavily armed forces faced each other. The state forces deployed cannons, trench mortars, machine guns, and gas grenades, although some questioned whether troops would fire on civilians if ordered. "I warn you, Huey Long, you cringing coward, that if a life is spent in the defense of this city and its right of self-government, you shall pay the penalty as other carpetbaggers had done before you," Walmsley threatened. During the standoff Allen summoned the legislature into special session to enact further legislation against New Orleans. After the governor sent 2,000 more troops to the city, a Baton Rouge attorney whose son was among them warned Huey that if his boy were hurt he would "kill you as I would any other mad dog."

Journalists reported on the spectacle of a state on the verge of war against a city; federal officials considered intervening. The FBI, which sent special agents to the scene, compiled 300 pages of reports, and summaries were sent daily to Marvin McIntyre, Roosevelt's appointment secretary. The president wanted to act if he could find a plausible justification: He thought about taking action to enforce the constitutional guarantee of a republican form of government in all states. However, FBI Director J. Edgar Hoover considered intervention unwise and acknowledged demands for action by writing, "No investigation warranted because no federal law violated." The president decided to let the situation run its course. "Roosevelt is no damn fool," Huey boasted. "He knows his place."

Despite predictions of violence, election day was calm and the Long candidates won easily. The New Orleans congressional delegation supported Long, who was also gratified by the election of his friend Archie Higgins of New Orleans to the state Supreme Court. A second Supreme Court seat caused problems. On September 9, two days before the election, the

Longite candidate, Winston Overton, died. State law specified that if a candidate died within seven days of a primary and only one opponent remained, the remaining candidate was to be the party nominee.

When the Democratic district committee met to designate Thomas Porter the nominee, Long showed up, took over the meeting, and had the committee reject Porter and ordered a new election on October 9. Porter obtained an injunction against the election and Long appealed to the state Supreme Court, which scheduled a hearing for November 26, more than a month after the election. Thus, Porter had to participate in the illegal election or be eliminated by the Long-controlled committee and court. Huey persuaded Lieutenant Governor Fournet to run for the position, and he defeated Porter. The court then canceled its hearing on the legality of the election on the grounds that the issue was moot. Long now knew the state's highest court would validate any laws his subservient legislature enacted.

A normal politician would have been satisfied; instead, Long had Allen summon special sessions in November and December. He suggested that he might "run the state" while Allen took a vacation and in November he facetiously suggested that Louisiana secede from the Union and annex the Mississippi Valley, boasting: "There's never been anything like this in the history of the world." The special sessions solidified Long's dictatorship; the November session enacted 44 bills in six days, followed by 33 bills in five days in December.

One bill created a civil service commission that controlled the hiring of policemen and firemen in every municipality. All nonelected municipal officials became state employees, meaning, for instance, that Walmsley could not hire his own secretary. Long summarily fired the Alexandria chief of police, who had stood by while he was pelted with eggs in 1933. Regulation of local utilities was transferred from cities to the state. Some bills were very specific; one reduced the salary of the district attorney in Baton Rouge, a Long opponent.

At the December session the state took over the hiring and firing of teachers from local school boards; the following summer anti-Long teachers were dismissed. Local sheriffs were limited to appointing no more than five deputies; additional deputies must be named by the state. The governor gained the power to appoint 13 representatives to the governing body of Baton Rouge and at its first meeting the new Longite majority dismissed all 225 city employees. Passing laws was becoming routine. Long had perfected a method to enact anything, to enforce it at his pleasure, and to have it sanctioned by state courts. Between July of 1934 and September of 1935 seven special sessions ground out the most repressive legislation in American history. Huey reflected that he had "the best legislature money could buy." Most bills were not even read, much less debated. All went to a single committee in each house, dominated by Longites; Huey ran the meeting while the chair simply sat. There were no witnesses for any bills and all were approved by identical margins. It was futile to object to or ask Long to explain the bills he proposed. An anti-Long legislator asked at one session, "When will we know what these bills are all about?" The senator replied, "Tuesday, when they are passed."

No bill was considered on merit; all that mattered was Long's will. By the end of 1934 an overwhelming majority of the legislators were handpicked robots. "I'm mighty proud to be Long's lieutenant," Allen remarked. "All the brains and energy that go into the running of the state come from him." Long dismissed charges that he was a dictator: "A perfect democracy can come close to looking like a dictatorship."

Long enjoyed flaunting his power. At one meeting of the House Ways and Means Committee he explained a patronage measure to permit the Long machine to appoint 30 additional employees in the office of the New Orleans tax collector. "This is a very charitable law," he said. "It gives the gentlemen down in New Orleans the advantage of the best talent available. It relieves the heart of Mr. Montgomery [the tax collector] of a heavy burden."

One of the two anti-Long members on the 17-member committee asked, "Has he requested the change?"

"Not yet," Huey replied, "we just anticipated that."

"Do you think he will like it?"

"He will have to like it."

The legislature set records for efficiency. On one day the House passed 44 bills in 22 minutes. Between August 1934 and September 1935, the seven special sessions passed 463 bills, almost all of which increased Long's power. Never had a legislature been so subservient to one man. "They say they don't like my methods," Huey told a reporter. "Well, I don't like them either. I'll be frank with you. I really don't like to have to do the things the way I do. I'd much rather get up before a legislature and say, 'Now this is a good law; it's for the benefit of the people, and I'd like you to vote for it in the interest of the public welfare.' Only I know laws ain't made that way. You've got to fight fire with fire."

Long pursued power compulsively. "First you come into power—POWER—and then you can do things," he rationalized. "The end justifies the means. I would do it some other way if there was time or if it wasn't necessary to do it this way."

The Kingfish was never satisfied. National observers were stunned by the willingness of Louisianans to exchange favors for political freedom. "They do not merely vote for him, they worship the ground he walks on," a national correspondent wrote. One woman said, "He is ... an angel, sent by God." After Long's death, one Louisianan reflected, "Huey Long was the bestest man we ever had."

Raymond Gram Swing, who observed fascism in Europe, was puzzled by legislators who supinely accepted Long's domination. "Psychology explains the dictators of Europe as appealing to the innate yearning for father-authority in most people," he wrote. "But Huey Long is no father-figure. He is a grown-up bad boy."

Many Louisianans turned to Long because they were desperate. A young LSU instructor told Swing, "There are many things Huey does that I don't approve of. But on the whole he has done a great deal of good. And if I had to choose between him without democracy and getting back the old crowd, without the good he has done, I should choose Huey. After all, democracy isn't any good if it doesn't work. Do you really think freedom is so important?"

Journalists and politicians compared Long to his contemporaries, Hitler and Mussolini. When Farley met Mussolini in Rome he immediately thought of Long. Lawrence Dennis, a Harvard-educated fascist, hailed Long as "the nearest approach to a national fascist leader" in the United States. "It takes a man like Long to lead the masses," he said. "I think Long's smarter than Hitler but he needs a good brain trust."

Long justified his methods by listing his accomplishments. His defenders talked about what he did, his enemies about how he did it. Although Long denied that he was a fascist or a dictator, some pointed out that when he said "A man is not a dictator when he does the will of the people," he was expressing one of the fundamental tenets of fascism, a mystical bond between the leader and the led. Also, like Hitler and Mussolini, Long inspired the masses to submerge their collective will in his.

Clearly, aspects of Long's rule resembled fascism: the demand for submission to a leader, suppression of dissent, scapegoating, emotional oratory, alteration but preservation of capitalism, and emphasis on ends rather than means. Long lacked certain characteristics of the classic European fascist, yet he possessed more such attributes than any American political leader with comparable power. However, whether Long was a fascist dictator or merely a very powerful rural boss, the distinction meant little to the people of Louisiana.

Long's defenders argued that his power originated in the people, and that he gave them tangible benefits in exchange for votes. Even his opponents in the 1930s admitted that a majority of Louisiana voters supported him. Nonetheless, he won only one election, in 1928, that was not to some degree rigged. Moreover, had Long believed his popular support secure, he would not have needed the punitive laws his legislature enacted in 1934 and 1935.

Louisiana had been reduced to a fiefdom by the end of the special session of November 1934, but Long was not content. Near the end of the December special session a bill providing for the codification of existing license laws passed the House and Senate committees and was approved by the entire House.

Shortly before the vote on the Senate floor, an administration senator offered an amendment 100 pages long. The secretary of the Senate mumbled a few words about the amendment, it passed easily, and was rushed to the House, which also approved it. Only afterward did legislators learn that they had enacted the same bill that had precipitated Long's impeachment in 1929—a five-cent-per-barrel tax on refined oil.

Huey humiliated Standard Oil and the city of Baton Rouge. Shortly after the bill passed, Standard dismissed 3,800 employees at its Baton Rouge refinery. Angry citizens, many of them fired workers, met in January and created the Square Deal Association to combat Long. The movement, led by former Standard employee Ernest Bourgeois, grew into a statewide organization; former governors Parker, Sanders, and Pleasant joined and women created an auxiliary. The Square Dealers armed themselves and drilled. Long planted a spy, Sidney Songy, in the Baton Rouge chapter, and secretly negotiated with Standard officials to arrange a settlement on his terms. Standard agreed that in return for Long's promise to reduce the tax to one cent it would use Louisiana oil for 80 percent of its refining and would fire or refuse to hire the leaders of the association.

Huey announced the compromise on January 22, but it did not end the Square Deal movement. On January 25, some 300 armed Square Dealers seized the Baton Rouge courthouse in response to the rumor that a Square Dealer had been arrested and was being compelled to testify about an attempt to assassinate Long; ironically, the man in custody was Songy. Allen declared martial law and the Square Dealers yielded the courthouse after a few hours.

The following day 100 armed Square Dealers assembled at the Baton Rouge airport, where they confronted 500 members of the National Guard, who dispersed them with tear gas and arrested their leaders. A few days later Long opened public hearings about the plot to assassinate him. Songy, the star witness, testified that Long's enemies had raised $100,000 to hire assassins to machine-gun him as he slowed to round "dead man's curve" on the Airline Highway between Baton Rouge and New Orleans. The hearings dragged on for weeks without incident or prosecutions. Baton Rouge remained under martial law for five months.

On February 26, a special session convened to implement Long's agreement with Standard. The legislature passed a resolution authorizing the governor to suspend any portion of the petroleum tax and Allen temporarily fixed the tax at one cent per barrel; if Standard did not behave, the governor could raise the tax. Altogether, the session enacted 86 of Long's bills, 22 of them in a single hour. Nor was that the end: Special sessions were called in April and July.

The July session further penalized New Orleans. The state prohibited the city from levying occupational taxes and nullified existing ones, took over the collection of the city gasoline tax and transferred collection of traffic fines from the mayor to the city police, who had become state employees. At the same time the state mandated higher salaries for certain municipal employees, hired by the state but paid by the city. New Orleans headed for bankruptcy and businessmen sought an end to the civil war on Long's terms. After the July session the Old Regular ward leaders abandoned Walmsley and asked for peace. Long's price was Walmsley's resignation, which was tendered after the Kingfish's death.

Huey's opponents were demoralized. "We lived under a government that was despotic and powerful and ruthless," one anti-Long legislator complained later. "It had the power to favor and harass: to make and break banks; to drive industry out of the state or to catapult it into great and illicit wealth, as it chose. By whim or caprice men and women were denied the right to practice their trades and professions; or the machine's favorites were granted these rights without regard to their qualifications or ability."

Moreover, the future did not look promising because no compelling anti-Long candidate had mass appeal. "I truly wish that we had been a more colorful group," anti-Long state Senator Jacob S. Landry said. Defeated in the legislature, the courts, and in elections, some came to believe that the only way to remove Long was by assassination. "There are many sane, thoughtful citizens who believe that only through a .45 can the state regain its political and economic sanity," Carter wrote.

Others felt that less drastic means would suffice. On July 24, 1935, several hundred anti-Long Democrats met at the DeSoto Hotel in New Orleans to plan a program to combat Long and to select a ticket for the 1936 state elections. Their only hope of defeating Long was federal patronage and, perhaps, federal criminal prosecutions of Longites. But Long, triumphant in Louisiana, did not fear Roosevelt. Rather, he looked forward to the opportunity to challenge FDR in the presidential election of 1936.

CHAPTER EIGHT

Kingfish for President

❖
❖

Shortly after his marriage in 1916 Huey Long told his wife that he had mapped out his political career—election to a secondary state position, then governor, senator, and president. By 1933 Louisianans had learned not to dismiss Long's prophecies. When Long ordered construction of a new governor's mansion in 1928, he built a replica of the White House. "I want to be used to the White House when I get there," he said.

Early in 1930 former President Calvin Coolidge visited the Louisiana governor. As they posed for pictures, Huey told the photographer: "Sonny, you have just taken a picture of an ex-president of the United States and a future one."

During his campaign for the Senate, Huey told reporters he was "headed for the White House." Two days after his victory signs sprouted on houses, barns, trees, and telephone poles: "Long for President." A huge banner across the highway leading into New Orleans read: "Huey P. Long, President of the United States in 1936."

The Kingfish wanted to revolutionize American politics through sharing the wealth. "There's going to be a revolution in this country and I'm going to lead it," he told Walmsley. However, he told a reporter, "I would rather see my [Share Our Wealth] laws passed than be president. But the passage of those laws is the only way they can keep me from being president—unless I die."

Long, who had bided his time in 1932, looked ahead to the

1936 campaign. "No man has ever been president of the United States more than two terms," he told Forrest Davis. "But when I get in, I'm going to abolish the Electoral College, have universal suffrage, and I defy any son-of-a-bitch to get me out in under four terms."

In 1935 Roosevelt blocked Huey's path to the White House. Disappointed because he believed the president paid him too little attention, Long accused Roosevelt of ingratitude: "I was elected without his help and he couldn't have been elected without mine." Roosevelt and Long both relished power and there was not enough to go around. Roosevelt had charted his course to the White House with as much calculation as Long had, emulating the career of his Uncle Theodore. The hillbilly from Louisiana and the aristocrat from New York were competitors with colossal egos. If Roosevelt had a more serene temperament, Long had a more brilliant mind. If Roosevelt had a second-rate mind but a first-rate temperament, just the opposite was true of Long.

Fueling the competition, Long and Roosevelt belonged to the same party and competed for the same constituency: the poor. Both were strong, decisive, and vindictive. "I have an unfortunately long memory and I am not forgetting either our enemies or our objectives," Roosevelt wrote. Long's success in destroying his political enemies was fanatical; Roosevelt's revenge was silent, steely, and cold, masked with social amenities. Long was more direct and brutal; nothing gave him more satisfaction than to see an enemy suffer.

Their enmity bordered on hatred because any increase in power for one came at the expense of the other. Long's resentment of the president, though, was almost pathological. "He really believed that anyone with a physical infirmity was bad or affected in other ways," Longite Lesley Gardiner commented. "He would quote the Bible to the effect God had put his mark on such people. I have heard him . . . say this about FDR." Another Longite said he had heard Long remark bitterly that Roosevelt was crippled in body and mind. Although senators and cabinet members customarily addressed Roosevelt as "Mr.

President," Huey alone called him "Frank," a gesture of contempt, not friendship.

Roosevelt was contemptuous of Long. Shortly after the Democratic convention in 1932, Roosevelt discussed political extremism with his aide, Rexford G. Tugwell. "It's all very well for us to laugh over Huey," he told Tugwell, "but actually we have to remember all the time that he is really one of the two most dangerous men in the country." (The other person, Tugwell assumed, was Father Charles E. Coughlin, the radio priest, but when Tugwell said so, Roosevelt replied, "Oh no, the other is Douglas MacArthur.") Roosevelt explained that there might be a revolution from the left led by Long or one from the right by MacArthur. Discussing the appeal of Long and other demagogues, Roosevelt wrote Henry L. Stimson, "In normal times, the radio and other appeals by them would not be effective. However, these are not normal times; the people are jumpy and ready to run after strange gods." FDR told his son Elliott after meeting with Huey, "That is a man totally without principle." Elliott said: "The Kingfish was no joke to my parent. To his keen eyes, Huey Long had much in common with Mussolini who, by promising the impossible, had made no scruples about the route he would choose to get there."

"If I could," the wheelchair-bound president told Joseph Kennedy, "the way I'd handle Huey Long would be physically. He's a physical coward. I've told my fellows up there that the way to deal with him is to frighten him. But they're more afraid of him than he is of them."

Long boasted that he alone dared to challenge Roosevelt. "I can take him," the Kingfish said. "He's a phony. I can out promise him and he knows it. People will believe me and they won't believe him. His mother's watching him and she won't let him go too far . . . He's living on inherited income." On another occasion Long ridiculed Roosevelt's intellect: "I'm as big as President Roosevelt. Why, he's copying my Share the Wealth speeches that I was writing when I was fourteen years old. So he's just now getting as smart as I was when I was in knee-breeches."

The two met only twice after Roosevelt's election, and, at first, FDR's persuasive abilities kept Long pacified. Long emerged encouraged from the meeting of January 1933. "I says to him, 'This is the Kingfish,' and then I said, 'I want a post office,'" Huey told reporters. "He said to me, 'I think you have a fair chance of getting it if you are right.' 'Well, I'm always right,'" Long concluded.

If Long had supported the New Deal programs in the Senate, Roosevelt probably would have funneled most of Louisiana's patronage through him. Huey would not have received all of it, because Roosevelt, a personal friend of John M. Parker and a few other anti-Long politicians in Louisiana, liked to spread benefits. However, after Long voted against the Emergency Banking Act, the Economy Act, the Civilian Conservation Corps, the National Industrial Recovery Act, and the Agricultural Adjustment Act, the president decided that Long was an unreliable ally and that he should support Huey's local opponents. He knew Long was unpopular with his Senate colleagues and might do more harm than good as an ally.

Late in July the president and the Kingfish met for the last time. Roosevelt had asked Farley to invite Long to the Oval Office to inform him that if he continued to oppose the New Deal the administration would give patronage to the anti-Long faction in Louisiana. It was a hot day and Long wore a white linen summer suit and a straw hat. He took a seat near the president's desk and began to talk, removing the hat only to emphasize points by rapping Roosevelt's knee with it. Farley and Marvin McIntyre, Roosevelt's appointment secretary, listened. Farley grew angry because he believed Long was deliberately disrespectful because he wore his hat indoors. Roosevelt, however, refused to let the snub annoy him, and the conversation was pleasant.

Huey claimed credit for electing Roosevelt and demanded patronage, but the president made it clear that none would be forthcoming if the Kingfish obstructed his program. Long became frustrated and emerged angry because the president showered him with charm but gave him nothing of substance.

"What the hell is the use of coming down to see this fellow? I can't win any decision over him," the Kingfish told Farley.

Neither Roosevelt nor Long was willing to permit use of patronage in Louisiana to build up the other's machine. Roosevelt did not reduce jobs or relief payments to Louisianans immediately, nor did he deny them to Longites. Instead, relief and public works were administered on a nonpartisan basis by the state director of the Federal Emergency Relief Administration (FERA), Harry Early. Both Longites and anti-Longites complained, although the New Deal helped the Louisiana economy.

During the winter of 1933–1934 some 325,611 Louisianans were supported by welfare checks or federal jobs, ranking the state sixteenth in the country. Federal aid was supposed to be administered on the basis of $1 for each $3 the state spent, but Louisiana contributed nothing. In April Early warned that "no state, however poor, however debt-ridden, can afford to take the position that it can do nothing and make no effort." A month later Harry Hopkins warned Allen that federal funding would stop unless Louisiana contributed its share.

Despite Long's promise to construct a modern highway system and his bond issues to build roads, Louisiana rejected half of the federal funds appropriated for highway construction. Long instructed his puppets in the state government to refuse any money they could not control and in the Senate he opposed measures designed to provide jobs and pensions, claiming they were inadequate. "For all his pleas on behalf of the suffering, Huey was uninterested in depression cures he did not originate," biographer Stan Opotowski wrote. "He fought many reforms because they did not go far enough, but his vote against them counted just as much as the votes of those who wanted no reforms at all." The struggle over the administration of relief was unequal: Roosevelt controlled about four times as many jobs and welfare payments as Long. The Louisiana economy benefited from federal money despite Long's obstruction. The FERA employed 70,000 workers in New Orleans alone by 1935, and between 1935 and 1939 the Civilian Conservation Corps, which planted in Louisiana the second-highest number of trees of any state, employed 42,000 young men. Federal funds paid teachers to instruct adult illiterates and provided 50,000 children with meals, instruction, and immunizations. Federal aid boosted agricultural income in Louisiana from $59 million in 1932 to $129.9 million in 1937; farm bankruptcies declined and by 1936 the Soil Conservation and Domestic Allotment Act subsidized about 69 percent of Louisiana's cropland. From 1933 to 1939 Louisiana received more than $465 million in federal grants and $290 million in loans.

There were limits to Roosevelt's altruism, though; he disliked subsidizing a state whose senior senator was preparing to run against him in 1936. The president shifted from the nonpartisan use of federal funds to the manipulation of them to sustain Long's Louisiana opponents. By 1935 five of the state's eight congressmen had joined Roosevelt against Long. In February, 1935, the president began to dismiss federal administrators who were Long supporters, saying, "Anybody working for Huey Long is not working for us." Federal agencies became refuges for Long's state opponents. The Home Owners' Loan Corporation hired his estranged brother, Earl, and Roosevelt consulted Sanders and Parker about Louisiana appointments. He made recess appointments to Louisiana positions to prevent Long from blocking Senate confirmation. And in April Roosevelt replaced the neutral Early with Frank H. Peterman, an anti-Long state senator, as FERA administrator. Workers Peterman hired were expected to be loyal to the New Deal. Finally, municipal governments wanting to challenge Long were told to apply for federal grants.

At a time when other states were begging for federal money, Louisiana rejected it. Huey did not want jobs he could not control. Long ordered the halt of construction of a $7 million bridge across the Mississippi River at New Orleans to prevent Secretary of Interior Harold Ickes from choosing the builders. Allen filed suit in state court to impound a $1.8 million federal grant to the New Orleans Sewerage and Water Board on the grounds that the state should administer it. The legislature passed a law prohibiting local borrowing of federal funds or acceptance of grants without state approval. Another bill provided that the Highway Commission advisory board supervise all federal money spent for highway construction. "This bill is harmless. All it does is to declare war on the United States," a Long opponent declared facetiously.

Ickes canceled public works projects planned for Louisiana: "We are certainly not going to give work relief funds to build up Senator Long's machine." Huey lashed back: "Ickes can go slap-damn to hell. If he had any sense, which of course he hasn't, or he wouldn't be in the Cabinet, he would praise this legislation." Ickes replied that Long was suffering from "halitosis of the intellect. That's presuming Emperor Long has an intellect."

More laws and recriminations followed. In July, 1935, the legislature made it a criminal offense to use federal money for political purposes. In August the Kingfish instructed his assistant, George Wallace, to draft a bill prohibiting any federal official in Louisiana from disbursing "any public funds appropriated or made available by the Congress," if Louisiana's government decided it encroached upon state rights. Offenders could be sentenced to 12 months in jail. When Wallace objected that such a bill was unconstitutional, Huey replied, "I don't give a damn. I want you to draw it up anyway."

Long also struck at Roosevelt by demanding an investigation of his closest adviser, Postmaster General Farley. In attacking Farley, who was also chairman of the Democratic National Committee and the chief patronage dispenser for Roosevelt, Long was employing a tactic he had used since he entered politics: The quickest way to establish a reputation was to walk up and punch the biggest guy in town.

On February 11, 1935, Long delivered a speech entitled "Farley, a Menace to Clean Politics." Labeling the postmaster general a "demon political ringmaster, and political tyrant," he charged that Farley had used his position to enrich himself and help Roosevelt politically. Without documentation, Long recited a lengthy list of abuses. Farley, he said, had a financial interest in a building supply company that profited from government contracts, compelled businessmen seeking contracts to contribute to the party, and extorted contributions from federal employees. Farley, he continued, was affiliated with a wire service that provided information to gamblers, and had given away stamps worth $80,000.

The charges were serious and Farley was obviously guilty of political favoritism, although Long furnished no evidence for the more serious charges. Long intended to force Farley to resign and embarrass the president. "When we appoint a committee to investigate Farley we will never have to investigate him," he predicted. "He will quit."

Republicans welcomed the charges and the administration permitted a probe by the Senate Post Office Committee to avoid the appearance of a cover-up. The committee, with a majority of Roosevelt partisans, was unlikely to vote for sanctions without evidence. Farley, pretending to be unconcerned, denied the charges.

Throughout the spring Long denounced Farley, terming him "just an ordinary crook." He intercepted a copy of Farley's rebuttal and read from it on the Senate floor. On March 8, the committee voted not to conduct a full investigation in the absence of written evidence. On May 13, Long delivered another tirade and called for a floor vote on an investigation. The following day the Senate rejected his motion, 62–20, almost entirely along party lines. Only two Democrats supported the motion; only three Republicans opposed it.

Unable to defeat New Deal legislation, Long used his oratorical skill to ridicule the administration and delay consideration of important bills with one-man filibusters. In 1935 his five filibusters annoyed his colleagues but entertained the galleries. Republicans rejoiced at the internecine warfare. In March Long attached a prevailing-wage amendment to the $4.9 million work-relief bill, then delayed consideration of the bill. It passed overwhelmingly without the amendment. New Dealers pointed out the hypocrisy of Long's professed sympathy for labor; in Louisiana he had prevented legislative consideration of a prevailing-wage bill.

Long nearly set a Senate record when he took the floor on June 12 to filibuster against an extension of a revised version of the National Recovery Act and spoke for 15 hours and 40 minutes. His talk was spiced with invective, humor, and digressions; Long read the Constitution, gave biographical sketches of Frederick the Great and Judah P. Benjamin, and stated his recipe for Roquefort salad dressing. When senators dozed in their seats or ignored him, he complained to the presiding officer, "I desire to ask that every Senator be made to stay here and listen to me unless he has himself excused." Garner replied, "In the opinion of the present occupant of the chair, that would be unusual cruelty under the Bill of Rights."

Long's speech amused Republicans. The NRA, he said, stood for "National Racketeers' Arrangement," "Nuts Running America," and "Never Roosevelt Again." Long offered himself for president. "If the present president keeps on going as he's going now, I may have to take it," he said. "And if the Republicans offer no strong candidate, I'll be almost unanimously elected." He might run as a third-party candidate. "You let the Democrats nominate Roosevelt and the Republicans nominate Hoover and we will beat them both put together so dad gummed bad you will not know that either one of them is running."

Democrats kept a quorum present and rejected Huey's requests to adjourn. Long finally yielded the floor and raced for the men's room. The bill passed.

Huey staged his most vindictive filibuster in August 1935. Before adjourning at midnight on August 26, the Senate hoped to pass a supplementary appropriation bill to pay Social Security recipients and other pensioners because the fund was exhausted. Long held the floor and said he would block consideration of the measure unless the Senate approved amendments increasing price supports for cotton and wheat farmers. Senate leaders pointed out that there was no time for the House to concur in such amendments; all Long would do was deny funds to the needy. Huey nonetheless talked until the session ended with no vote. The filibuster received enormous negative publicity. Because he could not get his way, Huey denied money to widows, orphans, the elderly, and retirees in the epitome of his determination to rule or to ruin.

Roosevelt considered it beneath his dignity to attack Long, but he encouraged his subordinates to do so. Early in March,

1935, General Hugh Johnson, former director of the National Recovery Administration, complained to the president that no one was answering Long's attacks and his hypocritical promises. Johnson offered to discredit Long and other administration critics in a speech at a New York banquet and before a national radio audience on March 4. Roosevelt agreed. Johnson was combative but no match for Long's eloquence. He called Long and Coughlin "political pied pipers."

Still, Johnson made some valid points. If poverty could be eradicated by schemes as simplistic as those Long and Coughlin proposed, it would have vanished generations ago. The dissident messiahs did not offer realistic alternatives to the New Deal; they exploited human misery by turning Americans against one another. Their opportunism would aggravate frustration and result in disillusionment. "They ask us to go with them gaily down pathways by them called new," Johnson said, "but that, in truth, have been trodden time and again in the world's history—but never to the rainbow's end they promise." Moreover, their demagoguery undermined democratic institutions. "These two men are raging up and down this land preaching not construction but destruction—not reform but revolution, not peace but—a sword." If Long did nationally what he had done in Louisiana, the result would be a fascist dictatorship. Huey was already "the Hitler of one of our sovereign states."

Roosevelt praised Johnson's courage, and congratulatory letters and telegrams poured in. Long was furious. The next day he rose in the Senate to condemn his critics. "There will be no more compromise," he vowed. "There will be no more shaking of hands." Robinson called Huey's invective a demonstration of "egotism, of arrogance, of ignorance," and predicted, "He may come to an end which he prophecies for others." The Kingfish treated his colleagues with contempt. "Why pay any attention to the ravings of one who anywhere else than in the Senate would be called a madman?" Long replied that he would not be intimidated by Robinson, Johnson, or the president. Neither patronage nor fear would change his message while people suffered; the only way to silence him was to adopt his program to end poverty.

The next day Long and Robinson renewed their debate. "Roosevelt has only a few millions more unemployed and only nine billions more debt than Hoover," Huey charged. Robinson confessed that if he had to listen to Long "criticizing and condemning everyone who does not agree with him," he wanted to leave the Senate. That gratified Long, who responded that Robinson's absence would encourage him to run for reelection. "God save the Senate," Robinson concluded.

Long demanded radio time to respond to Johnson's speech and NBC offered him 45 minutes. Although the subject of Johnson's speech had not been known in advance, everyone knew that oratorical fireworks would erupt when Huey delivered his rebuttal. Twenty-five million listeners tuned in and Long did not disappoint the largest audience of his career. He condemned the New Dealers as hard-hearted men who destroyed crops needed to feed the hungry through the destructive policies of the Agricultural Adjustment Administration: "So it has been that while millions have starved and gone naked; so it has been that while babies have cried and died for milk; so it has been that while people have begged for meat, and bread, Mr. Roosevelt's administration has sailed merrily along, plowing under and destroying the things to eat and wear."

The New Deal was fascist. The National Recovery Administration imposed more regimentation on business than Hitler. Johnson mimicked the European dictators by staging parades and utilizing symbols such as the Blue Eagle, much as Hitler used the swastika. More dangerous than the incompetent Hoover, Roosevelt lulled people into submission, then snatched their liberties. Hoover reminded him of a hoot owl, Roosevelt of a scrooch owl. "A hoot owl bangs into the roost and knocks the hen clean off, and catches her while she's falling. But a scrooch owl slips into the roost and scrooches up to the hen and talks softly to her. And the hen just falls in love with him, and the next thing you know there ain't no hen!"

The Kingfish dismissed Johnson as "one of those satellites loaned by Wall Street to run the government." The New Deal was a failure. "They have had their way," he said. "It is now worse than ever." For five minutes Huey subjected his opponents to withering ridicule; he devoted the remaining 40 min-

utes to a dispassionate discussion of his alternative, the Share
Our Wealth Society.

Long profited from the exchange. Johnson inadvertently
attracted an audience for Huey by linking Long with Coughlin,
whose followers identified with Long. Johnson poured gasoline
on Huey's fire.

The president had more effective means of undermining
Long's credibility. He orchestrated a movement by the Treasury Department and the FBI to investigate Huey and his associates for financial and political corruption. Even if they could
not convict Long before a Louisiana jury, indictments and a
public trial could thwart the Kingfish's ambitions. The corruption of the Long machine would be more difficult to conceal in
a national campaign than in Louisiana, where the machine
controlled the courts and the police and intimidated the press.
Elmer Irey, who conducted the investigation for the Treasury
Department, believed he had an airtight case, which was about
to go to a grand jury at the time of Huey's death.

Once a man of simple tastes, Long had come to love luxury.
By 1933 he owned a mansion in an exclusive section of New
Orleans worth between $40,000 and $60,000. He had a cash
annuity worth $100,000 with the Sun Life Insurance Company
of Montreal, a fleet of six Cadillacs costing $5,000 each, sound
trucks for campaigning, and a $3,000 wardrobe of imported
suits. Over the next two years he doubled or tripled his net
worth. At his death in 1935 the Baton Rouge *State Times* estimated his assets at between $2 million and $5 million. His
succession records declared assets of only $115,000 plus oil
stock, but it was common knowledge that Huey had a hoard of
cash. He lived lavishly and flaunted his wealth, sometimes
flashing $1,000 bills and telling a friend in 1935 that he "was
lousy with money." Dissolute in his habits, he saved little for
retirement, confident that he would be taken care of. Long
aroused suspicion by refusing to provide records and mixing
personal and political funds.

Caring more for power than money, he nonetheless manipulated money to attain power. It is likely that Long broke
laws by accepting bribes and kickbacks and not reporting his

income. He gave and took money in exchange for favors. Moreover, he corrupted those around him. Huey took graft throughout his career. Upon his election to the Senate, his opponents wrote dozens of letters to federal officials demanding an investigation into his finances. In 1931 Irey directed Archie Buford, his Dallas agent, to look into the finances of Long and his associates to determine if an investigation were justified. "Chief, Louisiana is crawling," Buford reported. "Long and his gang are stealing everything in the state . . . and they're not paying taxes on the loot."

Irey sent 32 of his 200 agents to Louisiana. After the 1932 presidential election, Treasury Secretary Ogden Mills instructed him to suspend the investigation and let the Democratic administration handle it. Roosevelt initially chose to ignore the evidence because he wanted Long as an ally, but after he broke with the Kingfish the investigation resumed. Irey, appalled at the documented corruption, concluded, on the basis of staff reports, "that practically every contract let in Louisiana since Long became Governor had been graft-ridden."

Irey came to believe that behind his humanitarian pretensions, Long was a con artist who needed the trust and friendship of his victims. "Huey's victims, the people of Louisiana, loved him," Irey explained. Another absolute necessity for successful confidence operations is ruthlessness, because bankers won't buy gold bricks but widows will. Huey Long was conscienceless.

Irey's strategy was to indict and convict Long's subordinates first, preparing public opinion for Huey's trial. In 1933 state legislators Joseph and Jules Fisher were convicted of income-tax evasion and sentenced to federal prison. Seymour Weiss and Abe Shushan were indicted, although neither was tried before Long's death.

Irey believed that even Louisianans would be shocked by Huey's manipulation of public oil leases through the Win or Lose Oil Company, incorporated by Weiss, Earl Christenberry, and James A. Noe with only $200 in capital. Long, a silent partner, held 31 shares and was the attorney for Win or Lose, a prototype for dozens of dummy corporations established during the Long regime; the corporations siphoned profits from oil deposits to political cronies. The concept was simple. Land was leased to individuals who created exploration companies that existed solely for that purpose. Because they invested only where deposits were already found, such companies as Win or Lose never lost. The exploration company, actually a lease trading company, obtained rights from the state for a pittance, sometimes only a few cents per acre, and promptly subleased to bona fide oil companies for hundreds of thousands of dollars plus a percentage of production. (In 1991 Win or Lose lands were still producing.) Profits that should have gone to the state went to Long and his cronies. The most successful of Long's lieutenants, Leander Perez, without apparent means, amassed a fortune of about $100 million. The Win or Lose royalties amounted to $320,000 in the company's first year of existence. Long's share was a $62,000 check, made out to "cash."

The deception that Irey unearthed was modest. In July, 1971, a New Orleans oilman filed suit charging that Win or Lose had diverted $250 million in royalties that should have gone to the state. Win or Lose eventually settled the suit by paying the state $200 million over 10 years.

The politicians who controlled the public lands above Louisiana's fabulous oil wealth used their power not only to enrich themselves but to make or break oil companies. Huey and his cronies, through favoritism, converted the small Texas Company into the conglomerate Texaco. According to the *Wall Street Journal*, the fledgling Texas Company, which sent its dredges and drilling rigs into a million acres of coastal swamps, yielded Long's heirs millions of dollars in royalties, which are still rolling in.

Long initiated the method of defrauding the state and had he lived his wealth would have skyrocketed. The exploitation of resources continued for generations. Louisiana's mineral wealth, much of it on public land, should have made its citizens and its government rich, and financed an array of social services. Instead, so much of it was diverted into political plunder that Louisiana remained poor. By the 1980s, when the resources were depleted, production declined and the state economy collapsed, raising the unemployment rate and lowering the tax base. Long's legacy was the perpetual impoverishment of the people.

Perez and Jules Fisher were the chief culprits in the unconscionable exploitation of the fur industry. Long, who did not participate directly, permitted their activities. In the late 1920s, when fur coats were fashionable, Louisiana produced more fur than the rest of the nation combined, more even than Canada or Siberia. Trappers in the marshes could earn $2,000 to $4,000 during the 90-day trapping season. Then, within a few years while Long controlled the state government, the trappers were reduced to economic serfdom. Perez conceived the idea of secretly acquiring leases on trapping lands, gained a monopoly, and then gouged trappers for the right to trap. He organized trapping companies as silent partners while publicly posing as the friend of the trappers and serving as their attorney and financial adviser. When local men balked at skyrocketing fees, Perez imported workers from neighboring states and stationed armed guards in the swamps to protect his fiefdom. The local trappers rebelled, culminating in a shootout in the swamps called the "Trappers' War." Perez eventually sold out for a tidy profit; trapping was never again free or profitable for the people.

Perhaps the most unsavory relationship Long established was his friendship with mobster Frank Costello, who testified to the arrangement in 1940 and again in 1951 during the televised Kefauver Committee investigation into organized crime. In the early 1930s, Costello predicted the end of prohibition and the resultant unprofitability of bootlegging and began to focus his empire on gambling. When Mayor Fiorello LaGuardia prosecuted gamblers in New York City, Costello looked elsewhere and Huey invited him to install slot machines in Louisiana, promising protection from prosecution and from competitors. In return, a share of the profits was earmarked for the Long organization. By late 1935 Costello had installed 1,000 slot machines in New Orleans and surrounding parishes and had diversified into illegal off-track betting on horseracing; later, he added pinball operations. The gambling empire was expanded by Huey's successors and reached its zenith under Earl in the late 1940s and 1950s. Costello contributed more than $100,000 to Earl's campaign for governor in 1940 and more than $500,000 in 1948. Longism and organized crime formed a natural alliance.

Huey increased his fortune by serving as attorney for some of the large corporations he publicly condemned; in return, he helped to reduce their tax assessments. Long also served as attorney for state boards and commissions that paid him exorbitant fees for collecting back taxes even though the attorney general's office could have handled the cases without charge. Huey did not deny his involvement; he boasted of it. "I admit that I'm the best lawyer in Louisiana, and I don't see why this state should not have a good lawyer," he said. But in fact, he delegated much of the work, which required no special expertise.

Long's vulnerabilities in a national campaign were obvious. His national followers, who did not drive exclusively on Louisiana highways or hold Louisiana jobs, were not likely to tolerate corruption. The patronage Long wielded so effectively in Louisiana would have been useless in a national campaign.

Roosevelt's arsenal included a weapon more effective than patronage: He could sponsor legislation that would cut Long's appeal. In the spring and summer of 1935 the president did precisely that. Among the bills proposed by Roosevelt and enacted by Congress was the largest public works program in the nation's history, the Works Progress Administration; the National Youth Administration; the National Labor Relations Act; the Social Security Act; the Public Utilities Holding Company Act; and the Wealth Tax Act. Roosevelt preempted his opponents on every front, offering employment, encouraging organized labor, providing pensions for the retired and the unemployed, breaking up monopolies, and levying the highest income, inheritance, gift, and corporate taxes in the nation's history.

Not all of the legislation was initiated by the president, and some programs, such as Social Security, had been under consideration since 1933. However, Long and the other critics of the administration influenced the timing and scope of the program. Roosevelt told Raymond Moley that he had to "steal Long's thunder." In May, while drafting the Wealth Tax Bill, he told a reporter that he was concerned about the political appeal of the Share Our Wealth plan. "To combat this and other crackpot ideas," he said, "it may be necessary to throw to the wolves the forty-six men who are reported to have incomes in excess of one million dollars a year." When he submitted the Wealth Tax to Congress he explained, "I am fighting Communism, Huey Longism, Coughlinism, Townsendism. I want to save our system, the capitalist system; to save it is to give some heed to world thought of today. I want to equalize the distribution of wealth."

Many journalists and politicians recognized that Roosevelt's motivation was political. The headline in the San Francisco *Chronicle* was "Roosevelt Urges Taxes in Share-Wealth Plan." And the New York *World Telegram* reported, "With one quick jab he seemed to puncture Huey Long's share-the-wealth balloon and rob the Louisiana Senator of his chief issue."

The measures placed Long on the defensive. If he opposed the legislation he would appear hypocritical; if he supported it he would find it difficult to differentiate between his program and the president's. The Kingfish tried to hold his followers by taking credit for the president's renewed commitment to liberalism and complaining that it did not go far enough. Roosevelt's bills were halfway measures designed to preserve an inequitable system by refining it. When the Wealth Tax bill reached the Senate, Long wrote Roosevelt, promising to help enact any law that would abolish economic disparities, but criticizing the bill as inadequate. Roosevelt ignored the letter; he neither wanted nor needed Long's aid.

Roosevelt was a tougher political foe than those Huey had defeated in Louisiana. Long could neither outflank him nor win a frontal assault. Although the Kingfish was eloquent, the president commanded a brain trust and a battery of speechwriters capable of overpowering a single speaker. Still, Roosevelt considered Long formidable. Therefore, he asked pollster Emile Hurja to determine how much support Huey might receive as a third-party candidate in 1936. Some 21,000 voters selected to represent different regions and constituencies were asked their preference among Roosevelt, Long, and other potential candidates. Roosevelt received the support of 54 percent of those who expressed a preference, 30 percent favored a Republican, and 11 percent preferred Long.

It was not the size of Long's vote, but its distribution, its potential for growth, and its ability to siphon votes—almost all his votes would come at the expense of Roosevelt—that alarmed the administration. The president and Huey would divide the liberal vote and the Republicans would win conservatives. In several large states, including New York, Long might poll enough liberal votes to enable the Republican to win. The Kingfish could be a nuisance.

Long doubted he could be elected president in 1936; his chief objective was to defeat Roosevelt. Huey thought of several possibilities: He might deprive either party of a majority and throw the election into the House, where he could trade his votes for influence, or he might engineer an incredible upset, much as he had by electing Caraway in Arkansas.

The Democrats feared Long's potential, not his immediate strength. A brilliant speaker, he had a campaign chest of several million dollars, some of it donated by wealthy Republicans who viewed him as a spoiler. Also, the election was a year away and the uncertain economy made the political situation volatile. As an individual Long was not a major threat, but if he could create a coalition among the critics of the New Deal, he would be a power broker. In the spring and summer of 1935 many pundits considered such a coalition possible; some analysts predicted a merger of the Long and Coughlin movements. Huey encouraged speculation by praising Coughlin and wooing his followers. "Father Coughlin is a good friend of mine," he said in April of 1935. Asked how his platform differed from Coughlin's, he replied: "Well, there isn't so much difference. I don't disagree with Father Coughlin very often; in fact, we disagree very seldom. Nor are our differences fundamental or important."

Roosevelt considered Long and Coughlin nuisances, yet he did not think it likely that they could create an organization that would threaten him seriously. "All these elements are flirting with Huey Long and probably financing him," he explained. "There is no doubt that it is all a dangerous situation, but when it comes to a show-down these fellows cannot all lie in the same bed and will fight among themselves with almost absolute certainty."

Long had not formulated his plans for the 1936 election, but throughout the spring and summer he sought support. He spoke to the Georgia legislature and a Republican meeting in Philadelphia, and toured South Carolina, where Gerald Smith was generating enthusiasm. He started to construct an airplane to tour the country and spoke on national radio networks eight times in the first seven months of 1935. He captivated farmers at Milo Reno's Farm Holiday Association convention in April in Des Moines, where a crowd of 10,000 applauded his attacks on the New Deal. He asserted that sharing the wealth was feasible: "Just addition, subtraction, multiplication and division will show you how it will work. Maybe somebody says 'I don't understand it.' Well, you don't have to. Just shut your damned eyes and believe it." He knew he had won the farmers. "That was one of the easiest audiences I ever won over," he said. "I could take this state like a whirlwind. What I did in Louisiana is nothing compared to what I could do in Iowa."

The Kingfish was confident that his oratory would win over national audiences. In 1935, he said of FDR, "I'm going to beat that son of a bitch." When Senator Wheeler expressed doubt, Long countered, "You've never seen the crowds I get." Wheeler replied, "But Huey, they come out to see you as a curiosity." Long agreed. "Yes, but when they get there—I get 'em!"

In the spring of 1935 Long conceived the idea of writing a novel to describe a utopia that would ensue after he became president. Ghostwritten by Christenberry and several journalists, it did not appear until after Long's death. *My First Days in the White House* described creation of a national Share Our Wealth Corporation, a huge mutual fund in which every American received stock. John D. Rockefeller served as chairman of the board, assisted by Andrew Mellon, who confessed that his wealth had become a burden. Huey's cabinet included Herbert Hoover as secretary of commerce and Franklin D. Roosevelt as secretary of the navy, a job that suited Roosevelt's abilities, Long explained. After Congress enacted his program and the Supreme Court approved it, he toured the nation to ask what more he could do. In response, a man in one crowd shouted, "Nothing! We have just found out how badly we needed you for President all the time."

Every major publisher Huey approached rejected the book; it was finally published by a minor press in Harrisburg, Pennsylvania, which insisted on cutting it by half.

Long altered his life-style to enhance his appeal to voters. From June 1934 to July 1935 he did not drink, and he permanently gave up cigars and cigarettes. He also dieted and exercised, reducing his weight from 200 pounds to about 175. Attempting to portray himself a family man, Long brought his wife Rose and his daughter, also named Rose, to Washington and New York. His wife gushed, "If everyone knew that man like we know him! He's so witty! He always sees the funny side of life, and he's so interested in his family—he phones us two or three times a week, no matter how important the things are that he is doing." Asked about politics, Rose replied: "I leave all that to my husband. Politics are out of my line. My chief interest is my family. So long as Huey still thinks I bake the best biscuits and pies in Louisiana—why, that's what keeps me happy and that's all I care about."

Long never tried to organize women opponents of Roosevelt and by neglecting to do so he missed a splendid opportunity. By late 1935 a variety of leaders, most of them on the right, willing to ally with any foes of the president, denounced Roosevelt in speeches, newsletters, and books. Elizabeth Dilling of Chicago, who wrote *The Red Network* and *Roosevelt's Red Record*, claimed that the New Deal was infested with communists. As foreign policy became increasingly important, isolationist women gravitated to Dilling and other opponents of the president, including Father Coughlin. As foot soldiers they did much of the organizing work of male opponents of the president; ultimately the women became generals in their own movements. Long was not only blind to the opportunity, he was actively hostile to political participation by women. He concentrated almost exclusively on organizing men, believing women would follow.

Lurking in the background was an issue Long virtually ignored—foreign policy. As a potential presidential candidate, Long's position should have been scrutinized carefully. Few candidates ever seriously considered for president were so ignorant about other nations. Al Smith's provincialism had embarrassed his party in 1928, but Smith was a worldly sophisticate in comparison to Long, who simply did not care about the rest of the world.

If elected president in 1940, Long would have been commander-in-chief when the United States entered World War II. He would have been a disaster as a war leader. He did not command international respect; most people abroad who had heard of him at all considered him a buffoon and could not imagine dealing with such an impulsive, undignified leader. Long could not delegate authority, take advice, or tolerate equals, which would have been fatal in wartime.

Long was defiantly proud of his ignorance of foreign cultures. He opposed the League of Nations, supported high tariffs, and never expressed interest in international trade, disarmament, or military alliances. He had little respect for generals, valued personal loyalty above ability, and had read little military or economic history. He never considered how his plan for American economic decentralization would fit into the world economy. Asked why he did not discuss the tariff, disarmament, or the League of Nations in his senatorial campaign, he responded: "League of Nations! What's that? There's only one public question that the voters consider in the state of Louisiana. The one question is Long or anti-Long. They either vote for Huey Long or they vote against him."

Long spoke in favor of high tariffs because he adamantly advocated protection for Louisiana products such as oil, cotton, and sugar. He advocated Philippine independence because its products competed with Louisiana's. To the extent he thought about foreign policy, Long was an isolationist. In *My First Days in the White House*, he wrote that his choice for secretary of state was Idaho Senator William H. Borah, one of the more isolationist members of Congress, who had taken an irreconcilable position against American membership in the League of Nations. In addition, Long joined Coughlin to lead a campaign that defeated ratification of American membership in the World Court in January 1935. "I do not intend to have these gentlemen whose names I cannot even pronounce, let alone spell, passing upon the rights of the American people," he said. "We are being rushed pell-mell to get into this World Court so that Senior Ab Jap or some other something from Japan can pass upon our controversies."

In *My First Days in the White House* Long also indicated that he would avoid foreign entanglements. He considered the Spanish-American War and World War I Wall Street conspiracies. "Let us get out of the entanglements of Europe and the Orient in the quickest way possible," he said. In the summer of 1934 Long spoke against American attempts to impose sanctions on Italy for invading Ethiopia, arguing against "action of any kind that will entangle us by cards of sympathy or by trade understandings, that will lead us into possible conflict, regardless of the merits or demerits of the cause."

Long really focused on 1940. He intended to challenge Roosevelt as a third-party candidate in 1936, or to run a surrogate and divert enough Democratic votes to engineer the election of a conservative Republican. A conservative administration would be a disaster, he believed, meaning that in 1940 voters would be ready for him. He would blackmail the Democrats into nominating him by threatening to run on a third-party ticket, ensuring another Republican victory. Until then, Long was willing to let the country suffer for four years.

Long had the Louisiana legislature change the date of the senatorial primary from September to January 1936 so he could win reelection and then campaign nationwide. His presidential candidacy was a long shot, but he had defied the odds all his life. Those who underestimated him did so at their peril.

CHAPTER NINE

Assassination and Legacy

❖
❖

Usually when Huey Long predicted he would become president he added, "unless someone kills me." Obsessed with his mortality, he felt he had to act quickly. Few expected him to live a long life. Even if he did not die violently, the furious pace of his life might have killed him. He was in poor health when he celebrated his forty-second birthday on August 30, 1935.

Huey, who genuinely feared being shot or stabbed, had been the first Louisiana governor to employ a bodyguard, and his protectors swelled to a legion. Fanatically devoted to him, they were not professionals, and were hired on the basis of loyalty rather than intelligence, marksmanship, or experience. Long never went anywhere without them. Long was not easy to protect, outwalking his bodyguards, changing directions impulsively. They trailed in his wake instead of encircling him.

Initially Long's fears of assassination were groundless. When he became governor he faced no organized opposition; most politicians and businessmen were neutral. By 1935 the situation had changed and many Louisianans, frustrated by the impotence of opposition, would have liked him dead. Among them were teachers fired because of their politics, property owners whose assessments had been raised out of spite, legislators who had been humiliated, and those whose businesses had been ruined. Even some of his own lieutenants who were publicly obsequious detested him. Some law-abiding citizens talked about assassinating Long, knowing they would die in the effort.

To discredit his enemies, Long encouraged speculation about plots. On two occasions he had Allen declare martial law in Baton Rouge on the basis of assassination rumors. Also, he claimed President Roosevelt would stop at nothing, including assassination, to eliminate him. For years, Long said, the Mellons, the Rockefellers, and the Standard Oil executives wanted him dead. Huey "cried wolf" so often that few people took him seriously.

In the spring and summer of 1935, as Long tightened his grip on Louisiana, some politicians predicted violence. In the special session in April, the Kingfish introduced a bill to provide for the appointment of poll commissioners by state officials, abolishing their selection by lot. His objective was the total elimination of local control over elections. During the debate, Representative Mason Spencer said on the House floor, "when this ugly thing is boiled down in its own juices, it disfranchises the white people of Louisiana. I am not gifted with second sight, nor did I see a spot of blood on the moon last night, but I can see blood on the polished marble of this capitol, for if you ride this thing through you will travel with the white horse of death." The bill passed, 61–27.

On July 21 and 22, a caucus of Long's opponents met at the DeSoto Hotel in New Orleans to map strategy to combat Huey and to select a ticket for the 1936 elections. About 150 opponents attended, including four congressmen, two former governors, five sheriffs, and a judge. The meeting was publicized and journalists attended. Long planted spies and on August 9 delivered a speech on the Senate floor in which he quoted from what he said was a transcript. "I would draw in a lottery to go out and kill Long," he quoted one man as saying. "It would take only one man, one gun, and one bullet." Another added, "I haven't the slightest doubt but that Roosevelt would pardon anyone who killed Long." Huey had portions of the transcript printed in the *Congressional Record* and in the *American Progress.* Those who attended the caucus admitted there was much loose talk about killing Long, but denied that there was any plot.

In September 1935, when Long returned to Louisiana to direct a special session, an atmosphere of hostility prevailed. A militant anti-Long group calling itself the Minute Men enrolled 10,000 armed members. On Sunday, September 8, Long drove from New Orleans to the Capitol despite the warning from his wife, who had a premonition of danger. Harvey Fields, Long's former law partner, drove 200 miles from Shreveport to warn the Kingfish that his life was in danger. Huey accepted suggestions to travel by a 'new route and to deploy additional state policemen and bodyguards at the Capitol.

Long spent Sunday afternoon conferring with state leaders. He introduced a bill to gerrymander the district of Judge Benjamin Henry Pavy and District Attorney Lee Garland of St. Landry Parish to ensure their defeat in the 1936 election. Pavy had been a district judge for 28 years and Garland, considered the more formidable politician, had held office for 44 years in St. Landry, one of the few parishes Huey was unable to control. Some of Long's assistants questioned the wisdom of the gerrymander, which gave one small parish its own judge, and limited four more populous parishes, including St. Landry, to a single judge. Long dismissed the objections and ordered the printing of several thousand flyers to smear Pavy and Garland.

Long also discussed candidates for the state ticket. At least six Longites believed Huey intended to select them for governor, but the caucus made no final decision. In the early evening Long retired to his penthouse apartment in the Capitol and dined with his bodyguards, then watched House proceedings. Huey sat near the speaker's podium and chatted with representatives, rising sporadically to walk to the governor's office. He seemed relaxed, almost bored; he told Earle Christenberry that when the session ended he planned a vacation with no itinerary and no bodyguards. At about 9:20 Charles E. Frampton, a friendly journalist, telephoned Long from the governor's office. He asked Huey, who was using the speaker's phone, if he cared to comment about a hurricane that had devastated southern Florida, killing hundreds of young men in the Florida Keys, many of them unemployed veterans working temporarily on federal public works. "Hell yes, I've got some comment. Mr. Roosevelt ought to be very happy tonight. Every soldier he gets killed is one less vote against him," Long retorted in a heavy-handed reminder that FDR had vetoed a veterans' bonus. Huey said he would join Frampton in the governor's suite to elaborate.

Long left the House and walked to the governor's office. When he got there, he looked in, failed to see those to whom he wanted to talk, and started back toward the House. As usual, Huey's bodyguards trailed; he walked too fast for them. As he started toward the House, a slender young man wearing a white linen suit approached him from the front. He was concealing a gun in his right hand beneath a Panama hat. John Fournet, with Long, thought the stranger appeared threatening and lunged at him, as did Huey's closest bodyguard, Murphy Roden. The stranger fired one shot at Huey point-blank, but Fournet deflected his aim from Long's heart to his abdomen. Roden grabbed the gun and wrestled the man to the floor, shooting him as he did. Huey screamed, leaped back, and started to run. He was still present, however, when the other bodyguards opened fire, emptying their guns as the assassin, killed by their first bullets, lay on the floor. "Give me a gun! Somebody give me a gun!" Allen, who was in the corridor, shouted. Then he raced to his office and yelled, "Close the door!"

A young reporter dashed into the press room in the basement and exclaimed: "They're shooting upstairs! They're killing everybody!" Concentrating on shooting Huey's assassin, his bodyguards lost track of the man they were hired to protect. Joe Messina was the first to realize that Long had disappeared. "Where's Huey? God, where's Huey?" he screamed.

Huey had run downstairs into the basement and Public Service Commissioner James P. O'Connor found him at the bottom of the stairs, spitting blood. O'Connor helped him outside, commandeered a stranger's car, and instructed him to drive to the nearest hospital, Our Lady of the Lake, minutes away. Huey's only words on the short drive were, "I wonder why he shot me?" At the hospital, O'Connor lifted Huey from the car and the stranger sped away without a word, his identity lost to history. A nun who was a nurse at the Catholic hospital helped to put Long in a wheelchair and push him to the emergency room. "How bad is it?" Huey asked.

"Shot cases are always serious," she replied. "It's best to be ready."

"Then pray for me, Sister."

"Yes, but you'll have to pray too," she replied. They did.

The word spread quickly that the Kingfish had been shot. Hundreds of curious Baton Rougeans drove to the hospital for a death watch, creating a massive traffic jam. Throughout Louisiana thousands prayed for the Kingfish to live; others prayed for him to die. In Baton Route, where Huey was unpopular, the mood was festive. Smith issued a press release requesting that "all 10,000,000 members of the Share Our Wealth Society spend at least five minutes in prayer" for Huey. Huey's three brothers arrived at the hospital. Julius told reporters that he was "sorry Huey was shot," but that "our government would probably be destroyed unless his political successes were stopped." Rose and the children drove from New Orleans, although they did not arrive until after Huey had slipped into a coma. Seymour Weiss also drove from New Orleans and arrived in time to speak to the Kingfish. Politicians packed the hospital.

Among the first physicians to arrive were Arthur Vidrine, whom Huey had plucked from obscurity to appoint superintendent of Charity Hospital, and Clarence Lorio, a family friend. Lorio told Long that the man who had shot him had been identified as a local physician, Carl Austin Weiss. "I don't even know him," Huey said. Vidrine, the senior physician, took control while other doctors were summoned. Huey told Vidrine that he would like Dr. Urban Maes of New Orleans to perform surgery; Vidrine called Maes and urged him to fly to Baton Rouge. Maes, joined by another specialist, Dr. James D. Rives, decided it would be quicker to drive the 90 miles. However, a few miles outside New Orleans a car pulled into their path, Rives swerved to avoid it and spun off the road. Their car disabled, Maes and Rives called for a tow truck and telephoned Vidrine that they would be delayed.

Huey had a small puncture in the abdomen and another in

his back. Vidrine believed the bullet had passed through his body. At first the Longites at the hospital were optimistic. "This is great," Smith remarked. "He's not going to die. He'll get well and what a fine piece of propaganda it'll make. The corporations have been trying to kill him, we've said. Now we can say—'You see.'"

Yet Long's condition deteriorated: His blood pressure dropped and his pulse rate soared, classic indicators of internal bleeding. He went into shock and lapsed in and out of consciousness. Despite the availability of equipment, the doctors did not x-ray Long's abdomen, but concluded that Huey's only hope was an immediate operation. Vidrine asked Long if he could perform surgery and Huey agreed.

Besides the six physicians assisting Vidrine, dozens of politicians were in the operating room, some only a few feet from Long. "I have thought then and have since, what a scene, here was a man dying and the room was full of politicians," said Long's friend Fred Dent. "I have often wondered how a bunch of politicians could have been allowed in a room like that when a man's life was at stake."

Lorio was even more emphatic. "It was a vaudeville show," he said. "Everybody that seemed to have a political ambition was lined up in that operating room." James O'Connor commented that a nun "was begging them to get out, but they were in there jumping around and everything else."

The operation lasted about an hour. Usually a physician repairing a gunshot wound traces the path of the bullet through tissue and attempts to suture internal bleeding. However, neither Vidrine—a competent surgeon who had spent more time as an administrator than as a practicing physician the last seven years—nor the physicians assisting him examined the right kidney, tested the bladder for blood in Huey's urine, or x-rayed Huey's abdomen. After Vidrine sewed up the wounded man, he continued to hemorrhage internally and ultimately bled to death.

The bungled operation doomed Long. In 1935, 65 percent of bullet wounds to the abdomen proved fatal, the patients usually dying from bleeding or infection. After the operation was completed, the specialists from New Orleans and elsewhere arrived. Maes asked Vidrine if he had catheterized the bladder and Vidrine admitted that he had not. Dr. Russell Stone examined the urine and found blood, evidence that Huey was still bleeding. The doctors administered five blood transfusions, but the blood simply spilled into the abdominal cavity from the injured kidney. They considered a second operation yet decided that Huey was too weak to survive further surgery. Despite the risks, they should have performed another operation; they probably would have killed Long in the process, but without surgery he was certain to die.

After the operation, Long was conscious only sporadically. Dozens of people wanted to speak to Huey and the doctors permitted them to try. Earl claimed to have reconciled with his estranged brother, but Huey hardly perceived Earl's presence. Seymour Weiss pressed Huey to reveal the location of the deduct box that contained several million dollars for Long's presidential campaign. He died without doing so, according to most witnesses. After his death every key on his ring was traced and none led to the elusive cash. Many Louisianans believe Weiss found the box and secretly kept the money; he bought three hotels and left an estate worth $7 million.

At 4:25 A.M. Long thrashed briefly in his oxygen tent and died. The consensus of those present is that he died silently, in a coma. "After Long died," O'Connor said, "the hangers-on all vanished. You never saw a place empty so fast." A pathologist was present although his wife Rose objected to an autopsy and none was performed.

Early Monday morning a reporter for the Baton Rouge *State-Times* knocked on the door of the assassin's parents and roused Mrs. Weiss. He asked her if she had a photograph of her son.

"My son? At this hour of the night?"

"Don't you know? He shot Huey Long. The bodyguards killed him."

Allen sobbed uncontrollably at a press conference that morning. "This marks the death of Huey P. Long," he said, "the passing of the greatest hero for the common right of all the people in America." The East Coast awoke to find extra editions of daily newspapers announcing the death of the Kingfish. Coughlin said, "The death of Senator Huey Long is the most regrettable thing in modern history." Socialist Norman Thomas viewed the assassination differently: "The death of Huey Long removes the ablest and most colorful forerunner of American fascism." Almost every major daily newspaper commented editorially and most abhorred the assassination but expressed little regret at Long's death. The Milwaukee *Sentinel* was typical: "No man can carry matters with so high a hand, no man can deliberately invite animosities and reprisals as Long has done without danger of raising some enemy who will adopt the tactics of the assassin." The legislature voted to bury Huey on the grounds of the Capitol, appointed a committee to design a monument, then passed the gerrymander bill. Rose Long asked Seymour Weiss to make arrangements for the funeral and he and Maestri purchased a $5,000 bronze casket and tuxedo for the body; few people had ever seen the senator wear formal clothes. The corpse was prepared for burial at the Welsh funeral home by the same undertaker who had prepared Carl Weiss's body.

Weiss was buried on Tuesday, September 10. His priest permitted a Catholic funeral on the grounds that his guilt in the murder of Long had not been established. Hundreds packed the church and thousands braved a thunderstorm to witness the interment at the grave site. Most did not know Weiss, but wanted to express support for the family. Almost every Baton Rouge physician attended the burial, and many of Long's opponents were present, including ex-governors Parker and Pleasant and Baton Rouge District Attorney John Fred Odom. The Weiss family received thousands of telegrams, many of them congratulating his parents for their son's act. The family rebuffed a movement to construct a monument to the assassin.

Long lay in state in the Capitol rotunda for two days and 80,000 mourners filed by his casket. No church services were held for the slain senator; the only ceremonies were at the grave site in the sunken garden on the capitol grounds. Weiss chose Smith to deliver the eulogy and Smith feverishly composed it, unable to sleep until it was complete. On Thursday afternoon,

September 12, 100,000 gathered for the ceremony. Long's father, exhausted, remained in his Baton Rouge hotel. Thousands of others who set out for the affair did not arrive on time due to a traffic jam that stretched ten miles. Soda peddlers did a brisk business and 200 persons fainted in the summer heat. Floral tributes covered three acres.

Seymour Weiss, Maestri, Allen, and Fournet bore the casket to the grave site, where Smith delivered the most eloquent sermon of his long career while flags fluttered at half-staff. "This place marks not the resting place of Huey Long," he said. "It marks only the burial place for his body. His spirit shall never rest as long as hungry bodies cry for food, as long as human frames stand naked, as long as homeless wretches haunt this land of plenty."

As the crowd departed, the LSU band played "Every Man a King," in slow time, as a dirge. Many Longites, although moved by Smith's oration, believed that he used the occasion to anoint himself Huey's successor. Weiss regretted giving him the opportunity, saying, "He capitalized on it, glorified himself." Russell Long added, "It was a political speech to himself." Smith, who printed 100,000 copies of his oration, was still giving them away 40 years later. "This oration has been recognized in the world of letters as one of the outstanding pieces of English literature of its kind," he proclaimed.

After the funeral attention focused on the assassin, his motives, and the circumstances of the shooting. Extensive hearings on the death of Carl Weiss examined rumors that Long had been killed by an errant bullet from one of his bodyguards. The first witness, Fournet, who had been at Long's side, gave a sober, factual account. Smith, called as the second witness, arose, trembling with fury, refused to be questioned by the district attorney, and called him a murder-plot conspirator. As Smith left the courtroom, Odom responded: "I care nothing for his opinion of me or my acts. But if he or anybody else says I engaged in any plot to kill Senator Huey Long, he is a willful, malicious and vicious liar."

No one ever credibly established the existence of a plot. Smith later claimed that Roosevelt had plotted to murder Long, working through Mississippi's Senator Theodore Bilbo. Bilbo retorted that Smith was "a contemptible, dirty, vicious, pusillanimous, with malice aforethought, damnable, self-made liar." Smith also claimed that Weiss had been present at the DeSoto Hotel conference where he had been selected as the assassin by drawing straws. Weiss, however, had been treating a patient at the time, ironically, a relative of Long. Through the years, as Smith grew bitter and paranoic, he hurled increasingly reckless charges. In 1972, seething with anti-Semitism, he wrote of Long's death, "He was murdered by a Jew and it is my belief that it grew out of a conspiratorial meeting for that purpose in Vienna, Austria, some months prior to the assassination." A few years before his death in 1976, Smith published a brief, fawning biography entitled *Huey P. Long: A Summary of Greatness; The Political Genius of the Century; An American Martyr.*

Carl Austin Weiss was not an alienated loser but a happy, contented man with a brilliant future. The son of a Baton Rouge doctor, Weiss, a talented student, became his high school's valedictorian, studied engineering briefly at LSU, then received a medical degree from Tulane. The Tulane yearbook wrote of him, "With knowledge aplenty and friends galore, he is bound to go out and make the world take notice." He received a scholarship to study abroad, one of only two New Orleans doctors to have won the honor. He studied for nearly two years in Vienna and Paris, then worked for two years at Bellevue Hospital in New York before returning to Baton Rouge to practice with his father in 1932.

In 1933 he married Louise Yvonne Pavy, the daughter of Judge Pavy. Both Pavys used their middle names; she was known as Yvonne, her father as Henry. Yvonne received a B.A. in French from Newcomb College in New Orleans, studied at the Sorbonne, and enrolled at LSU to pursue an M.A. She visited Adam Weiss for an eye problem and met his son. They dated, fell in love, and married. In June, three months before Long's assassination, a son was born and named after his father.

Weiss was quiet, although he was not eccentric, friendless, or narrow. He enjoyed sports, photography, painting, and especially music; he played in the Tulane band. He bought a handgun in Europe and enjoyed target practice but rarely hunted.

In the days before he shot Long, Weiss did not act like a man planning a murder. He bought new furniture and heating equipment for his house. On Sunday, September 9, he enjoyed a leisurely dinner with his family. They discussed the gerrymander bill, but not angrily. Yvonne, wanting her father to retire from politics, thought he could earn more money practicing law. That afternoon the Weisses and Carl's parents drove to the family camp on the Amite River, where they swam and played with the baby. After dinner that evening Weiss called a physician who was scheduled to assist him in surgery Monday morning. When he left his home that evening to visit patients, he expected to return, the evidence indicates.

Weiss never made any secret of his hatred of Huey Long. He had many reasons for detesting the Kingfish. Not only did Long plan to defeat his father-in-law, he circulated old unfounded rumors that the Pavy family had Negro blood. There was another sore spot, for Yvonne's uncle, a high-school principal, and her sister, a teacher, had been fired because they opposed Long.

Beyond personal vendettas, Weiss, who lived in Europe after Mussolini came to power and shortly before Hitler took power, believed Long a dangerous dictator. "He felt strongly that Huey was some menace to our democratic way of life and generally to the welfare of the state. He was very strong in his feelings that Huey was a very bad thing for Louisiana, that somebody ought to get rid of him in some way," said Carlos Spaht, a Baton Rouge attorney and family friend.

A quiet man, Weiss told his brother that he regretted his inability to express himself, or to get close to people. Yet Weiss was also emotional, despite his calm exterior. He had a temper, which he repressed with difficulty. Once, when some of his medical colleagues denounced Long's dictatorship, he began to cry. A few months before the death of Long, one of Weiss's patients asked him, "What's going to happen about this Huey Long mess?" Weiss's response surprised the patient. "All I know is, somebody's going to have to kill Huey Long." He paused, then added, "It just might be me."

When he left his wife Sunday night, Weiss probably had no intention of shooting Long. He had kept a gun in his car for several months since intruders had been found in his garage, and he always took the weapon on night calls, as did many Baton Rouge physicians. Weiss probably intended to see patients that night rather than go to the Capitol. If he had intended to confront Long at the Capitol, he probably would have walked rather than driven. The building was less than two blocks from his home and there was little chance of finding a parking place there while the legislature was in session. Weiss's route to the hospital would have taken him by the Capitol.

The explanation for what happened is possibly so simple that every Long biographer and every investigative reporter has overlooked it. When the police found Weiss's car on Monday morning, it was parked directly in front of the Capitol and out of gas. Since gasoline cost only a few cents a gallon in 1935, it is unlikely that anyone had siphoned the tank.

For Weiss to have parked where he did, he must have driven by the Capitol just as another car pulled out. His engine sputtering, he must have realized that he was out of gas. He went into the Capitol to seek help just as Long was walking down the hall; his temper snapped, and impulsively, Weiss shot him. Like many American assassinations, there was an element of chance: Had he arrived a few minutes earlier or later, he would not have encountered Long. At most times, the parking area in front of the Capitol would have been full.

This explanation is consistent with Weiss's state of mind when he left his home. "I am convinced beyond any doubt that my son did not go into the Capitol to kill Long," Adam Weiss said. "My son was too happy to think of doing what he is accused of trying, too brilliant, too good, too superbly happy with his wife and child, too much in love with them to want to end his life after such a murder. He would have known that it was suicide he was walking into, cold, deliberate self-destruction under the guns of bodyguards." His mother added: "His future was brilliant. He had the whole world in front of him." Weiss's younger brother said: "It was our impression that Carl was headed for the hospital to turn in his instruments to be sterilized for surgery scheduled the next morning. We felt this was his reason for leaving his home. What caused him to stop, what caused him to go, or to be brought or led into the Capitol, we don't know."

For more than 50 years historians discounted rumors that Long had been struck by a bullet from one of his bodyguards. Several authors of books about the assassination, however, believe the rumors are credible. In 1986 Merle Welsh, the mortician who prepared Long's body, told Ed Reed, who was writing a history of the assassination, that Dr. Vidrine had removed a .38 caliber bullet from Long at the hospital and that Dr. Lorio had removed a second bullet, .45 caliber, from Long's body at the funeral parlor. Lorio had gone to the funeral parlor because he was concerned about the lack of a thorough autopsy. It appeared to him that both punctures in Long's body were wounds of entry. In the presence of Welsh and other witnesses, Lorio searched for and found the second bullet. Welsh told essentially the same story to historian William Ivy Hair several years earlier. Welsh's account, if true, indicates that Long was shot by his bodyguards. Neither of the slugs removed would have fit Weiss's .32 caliber gun and witnesses agreed that Weiss had fired only once. Welsh's testimony is not conclusive—he was old and ill— but it lends credibility to the theory that Huey was slain by his bodyguards. Still, it is difficult to discount the testimony of numerous eyewitnesses—admittedly mostly Long's body-guards and close friends—that Weiss had fired his weapon at Long point blank. At a centennial conference on Long in 1993 three experts debated the assassination. Journalist David Zinman and publicist Reed argued that Weiss was not the assassin, but State Police Captain Don Moreau made a convincing case for Weiss as the killer.

The case of who killed Huey Long continues to fascinate and puzzle Louisianans.

Meanwhile, the Lousiana State Police reopened the investigation of the killing of Long. Weiss's gun, which had mysteriously disappeared, was found in the possession of Mabel Guerre Binnings, daughter of former State Police head Louis Guerre, who led the 1935 investigation. One spent .32-caliber bullet was found with the gun in Binnings' safe deposit box, and five unfired cartridges. Although there is no proof that the spent cartridge struck Long, researchers determined that the bullet had passed through a human body and then hit marble or concrete. Test firings indicated that the bullet could not have been fired by Weiss's weapon. This puzzled most experts, because Weiss had the only .32-caliber weapon known to be present at the shooting; the bodyguards carried higher-caliber weapons.

Long left two immediate legacies: the machine he established in Louisiana and the Share Our Wealth Society, a national organization. No one in the Long organization was capable of seizing the reins as his successor. The Longites, claiming Judge Richard Leche was Huey's choice and would complete his work, selected him as the 1936 gubernatorial candidate and paired him with Earl Long, the candidate for lieutenant governor. Leche, chosen because he was amiable, pliable, and unlikely to dictate to the other Longites, labeled the ticket of his chief rival, Congressman Cleveland Dear, the "Assassination Ticket." Dear, for his part, claimed a bodyguard had killed Long. The guard had been committed to a mental asylum, Dear said, where he spent his time muttering, "I killed my best friend."

Even by Louisiana standards, the issues raised were irrelevant. Leche described himself as "232 pounds of Huey P. Long candidate" and challenged Dear to "shoot it out with him with .44 caliber pistols." Smith employed a variety of oratorical gimmicks in his campaign for Leche. Dipping his hands in red dye, then holding them aloft, dripping, he declared that the opposition was guilty of shedding the Kingfish's blood, then summoned the voice of Huey from the heavens and Long replied, via a tape recorder attached to a loudspeaker in a tree.

Leche won 67 percent of the second primary vote, the highest percentage of any gubernatorial candidate in Louisiana's history. He was realistic enough to admit that the people had voted for a dead senator rather than a living governor. Virtually the entire Long ticket was swept into office, including Earl, now a power in his own right and bearer of the magical name.

Possessing all of Huey's powers without the liability of his megalomania, Leche intended to be a genial dictator, preserving many of Huey's laws but exercising them judiciously. Mayor Walmsley was compelled to resign as the price for repealing some of Huey's punitive legislation against New Orleans. Before Walmsley's resignation, Conservation Commissioner Maestri was appointed to the position second in line for mayor and he succeeded the New Orleans mayor. The machine compelled all potential opponents to withdraw from the mayoral election, and it was canceled. The legislature then added two years to Maestri's term. When he finally faced the voters for the first time six years later, Maestri lost to a young veteran, DeLesseps S. Morrison. Before that, the legislature showered money and favors on New Orleans and the taciturn mayor became a folk legend.

In October 1935, federal prosecutors tried Abe Shushan, a major Longite, for income tax evasion. His attorneys argued that the $400,000 Shushan had failed to report had been obtained illegally, hence, the money was not really his and he was not obligated to report it. The jury acquitted him, astounding Louisianans, including Shushan.

After Leche's impressive gubernatorial victory in January, the Roosevelt administration, desiring the support of the dominant faction in Louisiana at the national convention in June 1936, decided not to prosecute the remaining indicted Longites. If Shushan could not be convicted, no one could.

The real reason for the dismissals was a deal between the state and the administration, an arrangement so transparently opportunistic on both sides that it was labeled "the Second Louisiana Purchase." At the convention, Louisiana cast its 20 votes for Roosevelt and supported the president's proposal to eliminate the rule requiring a two-thirds majority for nomination. "There is no one now in Louisiana with national ambitions," Seymour Weiss explained.

New Deal money now poured into Louisiana, $100 million between 1936 and 1939. Roosevelt toured public works in New Orleans accompanied by Maestri; Attorney General Frank Murphy received an honorary degree from LSU; and FBI Director J.

Edgar Hoover was named an honorary general on Leche's staff. Gaston Porterie, the former attorney general whom the Louisiana Bar Association had expelled, was appointed a federal judge. Some Louisianans even believed Leche was presidential timber.

LSU became a political incubator for Huey's children. Daughter Rose was elected president of the women students, vice president of the student body, and campus darling; Russell was elected student body president. And the university became the focus of political plunder.

Huey had erected only 4 buildings, but Leche constructed 30, including an agricultural center larger than Madison Square Garden and a baseball stadium so commodious the New York Giants used it for spring training. Construction superintendent George Caldwell, who became a millionaire, built a luxurious home in Baton Rouge that was the envy of his colleagues in plunder, featuring a bathroom of black marble with genuine gold toilet and fixtures. Caldwell faked specifications, double-billed and stole LSU materials, then sold them back to the state. He also received a 2 percent kickback from every contractor who operated on campus. After his thievery was revealed, LSU President Troy H. Middleton, who succeeded James Smith, asked Caldwell, "George, didn't you know it was wrong to take that money?" He replied, "Major, I thought I was being a sucker. Some of the boys took 10% and I got only two."

James Smith was the biggest thief. He used food and materials intended for the university, received kickbacks, and invented fictitious minutes for the Board of Regents, authorizing increases that made him the highest-paid state official. Smith grew confident and bolder, attempting to corner the world market on wheat futures using LSU bonds for collateral; because there were not enough bonds to cover his investment, he had the LSU print shop run off additional ones. When the wheat market collapsed, and Smith lost the money, state and federal officials launched an investigation and Smith fled to Canada. Upon his capture and return he pleaded: "All I did, I did for LSU. I wanted to help out by earning some money."

In three years as governor, Leche reported $450,000 in income on an annual salary of $7,500. Flaunting $1,000 bills to pay for small expenses and constructing a mansion in the country, he said, "When I took the oath as governor I didn't take any vows of poverty."

Beneath the surface, a storm was brewing. Jimmy Noe, angry at being denied the machine's endorsement for governor in 1936, collected 980 affidavits documenting corruption and turned them over to federal officials. When a New Orleans newspaper reported about political deductions taken from state workers paid partly with federal funds, Leche quipped, "I deny the allegations and defy the alligators." Placed on the defensive, he explained that Huey had started such deductions. Why had not the newspapers complained then? The answer was obvious: Huey inspired fear.

Soon the entire state was awash in scandal and the blatant corruption abrogated the alliance with the New Deal. In 1939, Leche resigned under threat of impeachment. Federal prosecutor O. John Rogge, arriving to coordinate a massive investigation, said he would stay as long as necessary, which he anticipated would be one week. He remained eight months and 250 indictments were returned against state officials who had stolen an estimated $100 million. Leche, Weiss, James Smith, and lesser officials received stiff prison sentences. Three men indicted committed suicide before they could be tried; James Smith's attempts failed. When V. O. Key published his classic study, *Southern Politics in State and Nation*, in 1949, he entitled the chapter on Louisiana "The Seamy Side of Democracy." His opening sentence read, "Few would contest the proposition that among its professional politicians of the past two decades Louisiana has had more men who have been in jail, or who should have been, than any other American state."

The Louisiana Scandals of 1939 humbled, but did not destroy, the Long machine. Leche's resignation made Earl governor. "Better a little righteousness, than a great revenue without right," Earl announced sanctimoniously. Earl professed ignorance of the corruption, was not indicted, and ran for governor in 1940. His opponents argued that if he was indeed ignorant, he was too ignorant to be governor. Earl denied that all Longites were criminals, declaring that there were a few bad apples in every organization. Referring to James Smith, he said: "Smith is only one man. Don't blame everybody. Look at Jesus Christ. He picked twelve. And one of them was a son-of-a-gun!"

The anti-Long faction, seizing the initiative, pointed out sins of omission as well as commission. Despite Huey's campaign pledge to improve state mental hospitals, conditions had deteriorated. Forty-one hundred patients were packed into buildings designed for 2,500, and not a single building had been erected under Long, Allen, or Leche. The state paid only nine cents per inmate per day for food and patients had not received fresh fruit in three years, although the hospitals returned unspent money to the state, which used some of it to construct a football stadium.

Earl lost the 1940 election to reformer Sam Jones, who was succeeded by anti-Longite Jimmie Davis, but Earl defeated Jones in a rematch in 1948. Unable to succeed himself, Earl retired to farm in 1952, then won the first primary in the 1956 gubernatorial election. After a nervous breakdown, he was elected to Congress in 1960, but died before taking office. Earl's cousin Speedy won the congressional seat and in turn lost to another cousin, Gillis, who died and was succeeded by his widow, Cathy. Blanche, Earl's wife, served as national Democratic committeewoman and on the state tax commission. Huey's wife Rose completed his unexpired term in the Senate and son Russell was a U.S. Senator from 1948 to 1986. Huey's brother George served two terms in Congress.

Even those who voted against the Long machine did not repudiate Huey. A poll in 1940 revealed that 60 percent of voters thought state elections dishonest; only 25 percent considered them honest and 15 percent had no opinion. Some people would not even talk to pollsters for fear of reprisals. But when the pollsters asked whether Huey Long had been a good or bad influence in Louisiana, 55 percent answered "good," 22 percent "bad," 14 percent "both good and bad," and 9 percent had no opinion.

The Long dynasty fed off Huey's legacy, although none of the candidates who followed him was his equal. For 25 years after Huey's death two factions dominated state politics: the Longs and the anti-Longs. The anti-Longs depicted the Longs as venal predators; the Longs responded that their opponents were vacuous reactionaries. Huey set the agenda that determined the political context for the entire period. No Long candidate who succeeded him was an original thinker although some were colorful personalities. Through the entire period, economic conditions in Louisiana improved marginally if at all. In 1930 Louisiana ranked thirty-ninth nationally in per capita income; in 1970 it ranked forty-fifth.

By 1960, bifactional politics had foundered on the issue of race. That year, for the first time since 1928, there was no candidate identified with the Long faction in the second gubernatorial primary. Later, the once-powerful faction survived only in folklore.

Longism was more than an ephemeral phenomenon, less than a permanent institution. Huey, in his greatest failure, did not institutionalize the revolution he tried to create. He changed the style of state politics more than its substance. By all objective criteria comparing the citizens of Louisiana to those in other states—percapita income, welfare benefits, years of education, literacy, and standard of living—they were no better off in 1990 than they were in 1928. Like Roosevelt, Huey provided hope for the impoverished, yet just as Roosevelt was unable to end the Depression, Long was unable to bring prosperity to his state. The United States went on to experience unprecedented prosperity after World War II; Louisiana sank back into a morass of poverty and political depravity. Long's national legacy is quite different. On the state level he furnished works without ideology; on the national level he provided ideology without works.

Long's lieutenant, Gerald Smith, was the only member of his organization with a national orientation. Smith probably was more sincere about sharing the wealth than Long, and unlike Long he actually believed it feasible. Huey's other lieutenants, most of them millionaires, had little sympathy for wealth sharing and little stomach for political combat on a national scale. "Share Our Wealth was a lot of bullshit," Maestri said after Long's death. "Hell, Huey only used it to get attention, but Smith wanted to take *my money* and give it to the poor!"

Unlike the other Longites, Smith never reconciled with Roosevelt. Fearing he might jeopardize their alliance with the New Deal after 1936, state leaders banished Smith from Louisiana, cutting off his salary and denying him access to the mailing list of the Share Our Wealth Society.

Smith tried to create the elusive anti-Roosevelt coalition that Long had envisioned. He drifted first to Georgia, where he sought a brief alliance with Governor Eugene Talmadge. When Talmadge failed to emerge as a serious candidate, Smith opportunistically attached himself to the pension movement of Townsend. In turn, they allied with Coughlin and announced the creation of the Union Party, which ran North Dakota Congressman William Lemke for president. A pale ghost of the vast coalition Long had dreamed of in 1935, the party created barely a ripple in the election. Lemke polled only 892,000 of about 45,000,000 votes cast, about 1.8 percent, and failed to carry a single state or to alter the outcome. Roosevelt trounced him and Republican candidate Alfred M. Landon by carrying every state except Maine and Vermont.

Smith drifted into the netherworld of anti-Semitism, published a hate-sheet, *The Cross and the Flag,* and toured the country exposing conspiracies that existed only in his demented imagination. He continued to attract large crowds until the 1950s and became a millionaire through contributions received in the mail. He used some of the money to build a towering statue of Jesus in Eureka Springs, Arkansas; to collect Bibles and antiques; raise goats and miniature horses; collect Christian art; and to stage an outdoor Passion Play. Smith, who still considered Huey Long his greatest hero, died in 1976.

Long's national following included many people who believed that Long, his offensive personality and dictatorship aside, had identified a major social evil and proposed a plausible solution. By attacking concentrated wealth and political power he appealed to a strain in America's agrarian tradition that was Jeffersonian and Jacksonian, perpetuated by the Populists of the 1890s, and described sentimentally by the Southern Agrarian poets. All of them believed that bigness threatened individual autonomy. Fortunes, and political and industrial power, had to be fragmented if their version of America was to survive.

Long was not the sole voice that challenged concentrated wealth and power; he was one of a chorus, perhaps the most effective member in his homely eloquence. In the final analysis, he represented not a liberal view of the future, but a rearguard attack on modernization. Unable to present a practical alternative to the economic behemoths, he turned his fire on the individuals who symbolized the wealth and power he resented. Yet bigness was not the sole enemy of prosperity; in fact, it was necessary for prosperity. Small banks foreclosed more frequently than large ones; little merchants were more likely to deny credit than chain stores; tiny entrepreneurs were more likely to pay slave wages than great industrialists. For Long to have admitted that the problem was complex institutions rather than evil individuals would have forced him to admit that there was no simple solution. His eloquence, while not entirely wasted, was misdirected; his cause was doomed by the course of modernization. Long lived in revolutionary times although he was not a revolutionary. For all his radical rhetoric, he was aligned with the forces of reaction.

Because he was slain while in his prime, he will be remembered for his promise and his potential. What he perceived to be a noble vision, or maybe only an avenue to national power, was an illusion more detrimental than the problems it was conceived to solve. Social justice cannot be dictatorially imposed on any level; that is the perennial promise and ultimate deception of dictators everywhere. The paradox of Huey Long is the paradox of America—of poverty amidst plenty, of promises unfulfilled, of eternal hope.

A Note on the Sources

❖
❖

Huey Long has been the subject of numerous biographies, popular and scholarly articles, and chapters of books about the South, the New Deal era, and American demagogues. Each biography has built upon previous ones in the absence of a large collection of Long papers. The more useful collections of documents are deposited at Louisiana State University, which houses a small collection of Long papers, most relating to his law practice, family, and early career. Highly useful are the massive Long scrapbooks, which document every phase of Long's career in detail. Also available at LSU are accounts of some of the 295 interviews that historian T. Harry Williams taped while researching his biography of Long. Unfortunately, the Williams collection is not nearly as useful as it might be. Instead of typing verbatim transcripts, Williams made only summaries of the interviews, then taped over the interviews with later ones, thus destroying some. Furthermore, the summaries are highly selective; for example, several hours of interviews with Cecil Morgan were compressed into a summary of about three pages.

There is a small collection of Long papers at the Perkins Library, Duke University. In addition, I obtained a file on Long from the Federal Bureau of Investigation under the Freedom of Information Act.

The Gerald L. K. Smith papers at the Bentley Historical Library, University of Michigan, provide a wealth of information on Smith, but little on Huey Long. The Sam Jones papers at the Howard-Tilton Memorial Library, Tulane University, have little direct bearing on Long. I also examined the Leander H. Perez papers, in possession of Perez's family in New Orleans, which include information on Long's finances and impeachment. There are scattered references to Long in the Franklin D. Roosevelt collection at the Roosevelt Library at Hyde Park, New York, and in the papers of New Dealers at various libraries.

Long's newspaper, the *Louisiana Progress* (called the *American Progress* after 1933) was a propaganda tool but provides information on Long's campaigns. Complete newspaper coverage of Long appeared in the Baton Rouge *Morning Advocate*, the Shreveport *Journal*, the *New York Times*, and in three New Orleans dailies, the *Times-Picayune, Item,* and *States*.

Long's autobiography, *Every Man a King* (New Orleans, 1933), is unreliable yet revealing of Long's view of himself. *My First Days in the White House* (Harrisburg, Pa.: Telegraph Press, 1935), an account of what he would have done as president, was published posthumously. There are several journalistic biographies written during Long's lifetime or shortly thereafter. These include Webster Smith, *The Kingfish: A Biography of Huey P. Long* (New York: G. P. Putnam's Sons, 1933); John Kingston Fineran, *The Career of a Tinpot Napoleon* (New Orleans: The author, 1933); Forrest Davis, *Huey Long: A Candid Biography* (New York: Dodge Publishing Co., 1935); Carleton Beals, *The Story of Huey P. Long* (Philadelphia: J. B. Lippincott Co., 1935); and Thomas O. Harris, *The Kingfish: Huey P. Long, Dictator* (New Orleans: Pelican Publishing Company, 1938). Of these, Beals's is the best-written and most reliable.

James A. Fortier, ed., *Huey Pierce Long: The Martyr of the Age* (New Orleans: n.p., 1937), contains eulogies to Long. Harnett T. Kane, *Louisiana Hayride: The American Rehearsal for Dictatorship, 1928–1940* (reprint ed.Gretna, La.: Pelican Publishing Company, 1971), is a journalistic indictment of the Long machine. Harvey G. Fields, *True History of the Life, Works, Assassination and Death of Huey Pierce Long* (n.p., 1945), praises Long. The first detailed scholarly treatment of Long and Longism was Allan P.

Sindler, *Huey Long's Louisiana: State Politics, 1920–1952* (Baltimore: Johns Hopkins University Press, 1956), a condemnation of Longs and anti-Longs.

Two journalistic accounts of the Long family appeared four years later: Stan Opotowsky, *The Longs of Louisiana* (New York: E. P. Dutton & Company, 1960), and Thomas Martin, *Dynasty: The Longs of Louisiana* (New York: G. P. Putnam's Sons, 1960). The most comprehensive study of Long is T. Harry Williams, *Huey Long* (New York: Alfred A. Knopf, 1969), a massively detailed account flawed by a tendency to excuse Long's excesses and a failure to place him in a state or national context. Glen Jeansonne, "The Apotheosis of Huey Long," *Biography*, 12 (Fall 1989) is a scathing critique of the Williams interpretation. Alan Brinkley, *Voices of Protest: Huey Long, Father Coughlin, and the Great Depression* (New York: Alfred A. Knopf, 1982), is a biography of Long and Father Charles E. Coughlin. Henry M. Christman, *Kingfish to America: Share Our Wealth* (New York: Schocken Books, 1985), is a collection of Long's speeches; David Malone, *Hattie and Huey: An Arkansas Tour* (Fayetteville, Ark.: University of Arkansas Press, 1989), is the most thorough account of Huey's campaign for Hattie Caraway. William Ivy Hair's *The Kingfish and His Realm: The Life and Times of Huey P. Long* (Baton Rouge: Louisiana State University Press, 1991), is the best single account of Long's life. The recent biographies are far more critical of Long than Williams's.

Several books have examined Long's assassination: Hermann Deutsch, *The Huey Long Murder Case* (Garden City, N.Y.: Doubleday, 1963); David H. Zinman, *The Day Huey Long was Shot* (New York: Ivan Obolensky, Inc., 1963); and Ed Reed, *Requiem for a Kingfish* (Baton Rouge: Award Publications, 1986). Reed is the most thorough and original.

Two collections of essays present a diversity of views on Long: Henry C. Dethloff, *Huey P. Long: Southern Demagogue or American Democrat?* (Lafayette, La.: USL History Series, 1976), and Hugh Davis Graham, *Huey Long* (Englewood Cliffs, N. J.: Prentice-Hall, Inc., 1970).

Of the dozens of scholarly articles on Long, among the more useful are Henry C. Dethloff, "Huey Pierce Long: Interpretations," *Louisiana Studies*, 3 (Summer 1964); John Moreau Adam, "Huey Long and His Chroniclers," *Louisiana History*, 6 (Spring 1965); Robert E. Snyder, "Huey Long and the Presidential Election of 1936," *Louisiana History*, 16 (Spring 1975); Dethloff, "The Longs: Revolution or Populist Retrenchment?" *Louisiana History*, 19 (Fall 1978); and Brinkley, "Huey Long, the Share Our Wealth Movement and the Limits of Depression Dissidence," *Louisiana History*, 22 (Spring 1981).

Articles on specialized aspects of Long's career include Robert E. Snyder, "The Concept of Demagoguery: Huey Long and His Literary Critics," *Louisiana Studies*, 15 (Spring 1976); Snyder, "Huey Long and the Cotton-Holiday Plan of 1931," *Louisiana History*, 18 (Summer 1974); Donald W. Whisenhunt, "Huey Long and the Texas Cotton Acreage Control Law of 1931," *Louisiana Studies*, 13 (Summer 1974); Michael L. Gillette, "Huey Long and the Chaco War," *Louisiana History*, 11 (Fall 1970); John R. Pleasant, Jr., "Ruffin G. Pleasant and Huey P. Long on the Prison-Stripe Controversy," *Louisiana History*, 15 (Fall 1974); and William F. Mugleston, "Cornpone and Potlikker: A Moment of Relief in the Great Depression," *Louisiana History*, 16 (Summer 1975).

In this book I have elaborated upon some of my earlier articles about Long, including "Political Corruption in Louisiana," *Louisiana Review*, 3 (Fall 1974); "Challenge to the New Deal: Huey P. Long and the Redistribution of the National Wealth," *Louisiana History*, 21 (Fall 1980); "What is the Legacy of the Longs?" *Louisiana Review*, 9 (Winter 1980); "Utopia Comes to the Masses: Huey P. Long's Share Our Wealth Society," in Ralph Aderman, ed., *The Quest for Social Justice* (Madison, Wis.: University of Wisconsin Press, 1982); "Longism: Mainstream Politics or Aberration? Louisiana Before and After Huey Long," *Mid-America*, 71 (April–July 1989); and "Huey P. Long: A Political Contradiction," *Louisiana History*, 31 (Winter 1990).

It is impossible to mention all the scholarly articles dealing indirectly with Long, but some of the better ones are Edward F. Haas, "New Orleans on the Half-Shell: The Maestri Era, 1936–1946," *Louisiana History*, 13 (Summer 1972); Matthew J. Schott,

"Class Conflict in Louisiana Voting Since 1877: Some New Perspectives," *Louisiana History*, 12 (Spring 1971); and Schott, "Death of Class Struggle: End of Louisiana History?" *Louisiana History*, 31 (Winter 1990). Several of my own articles are relevant, including "Preacher, Populist, Propagandist: The Early Career of Gerald L. K. Smith," *Biography*, 2 (Fall 1979); "Partisan Parson: An Oral History Account of the Louisiana Years of Gerald L. K. Smith," *Louisiana History*, 23 (Winter 1982); and "Oral History, Biography, and Political Demagoguery: The Case of Gerald L. K. Smith," *Oral History Review*, 11 (1981).

Huey's younger brother Earl is the subject of A. J. Liebling, *The Earl of Louisiana* (Baton Rouge: Louisiana State University Press, 1970), of Richard B. McCaughan, *Socks on a Rooster* (Baton Rouge: Claitor's Book Store, 1967), and of the superior biography by Michael L. Kurtz and Morgan D. Peoples, *Earl K. Long: The Saga of Uncle Earl and Louisiana Politics* (Baton Rouge: Louisiana State University Press, 1990). I have benefited from research for my biographies of Long's lieutenants, *Leander Perez: Boss of the Delta* (Baton Rouge: Louisiana State University Press, 1977), and *Gerald L. K. Smith: Minister of Hate* (New Haven, Conn.: Yale University Press, 1988), as well as from my *Race, Religion and Politics: The Louisiana Gubernatorial Elections of 1959–60* (Lafayette, La.: USL History Series, 1977). Smith wrote an autobiography, *Besieged Patriot* (Eureka Springs, Ark.: Elna M. Smith Foundation, 1978), and a fawning book about Long, *Huey P. Long: Summary of Greatness, Political Genius, American Martyr* (Eureka Springs, Ark.: Elna M. Smith Foundation, 1975). Both are largely products of Smith's imagination.

The best resource for sources on Longism and other aspects of Louisiana History is Light T. Cummins and Glen Jeansonne, eds., *A Guide to the History of Louisiana* (Westport, Conn.: Greenwood Press, 1982). My contribution, "The Age of Long and Beyond," surveys the literature in more detail than this essay but is somewhat dated. Students of Long can also learn from studies of other Louisiana politicians and aspects of state history, including Edward F. Haas, *DeLesseps S. Morrison and the Image of Reform: New Orleans Politics, 1946–1961* (Baton Rouge: Louisiana State University Press, 1974); Haas, *Political Leader-*

ship in a Southern City: New Orleans in the Progressive Era, 1896–1902 (Ruston, La.: McGinty Monographs, 1988); and Mark T. Carleton, *Politics and Punishment: A History of the Louisiana State Penal System* (Baton Rouge: Louisiana State University Press, 1971). Perry H. Howard, *Political Tendencies in Louisiana* (Baton Rouge: Louisiana State University Press, 1971), provides perspectives on state voting.

Two books about earlier periods in Louisiana's history are valuable: William Ivy Hair, *Bourbonism and Agrarian Protest: Louisiana Politics, 1877–1900* (Baton Rouge: Louisiana State University Press, 1969), and Roger W. Shugg, *Origins of Class Struggle in Louisiana* (Baton Rouge: Louisiana State University Press, 1939). However, the latter is dated and not entirely reliable.

Several books about the South, American demagoguery, and politics in the 1930s include accounts of Long. Among them are Franklin Hope Carter, *American Messiahs* (New York: Simon and Schuster, 1935); V. O. Key, *Southern Politics in State and Nation* (New York: Vintage Books, 1949); Isabel Leighton, ed., *The Aspirin Age, 1919–1941* (New York: Simon and Schuster, 1968); Reinhard H. Luthin, *American Demagogues* (Boston: Beacon Press, 1954); Alan A. Michie and Frank Rhylick, *Dixie Demagogues* (New York: Vanguard Press, 1939); Donald R. McCoy, *Angry Voices: Left of Center Politics in the New Deal Era* (Lawrence, Kan.: University of Kansas Press, 1958); Raymond Graham Swing, *Forerunners of American Fascism* (New York: Julian Messner, 1935); Alfred Steinberg, *The Bosses* (New York: MacMillan Company, 1972); and Studs Terkel, *Hard Times: An Oral History of the Great Depression* (New York: Avon Books, 1971).

Books about Roosevelt and his administration and memoirs of New Dealers include sections about Long. Useful are James MacGregor Burns, *Roosevelt: The Lion and the Fox* (New York: Harcourt Brace and Company, 1956); James A. Farley, *Behind the Ballots: The Personal History of a Politician* (New York: Harcourt Brace and Company, 1938); Elmer Irey and William J. Slocum, *The Tax Dodgers* (New York: Fireside Press, 1949); William E. Leuchtenberg, *Franklin D. Roosevelt and the New Deal* (New York: Harper & Row, 1963); Raymond Moley, *After Seven*

Years (New York: Funk & Wagnalls Company, 1939); Arthur M. Schlesinger, Jr., *The Age of Roosevelt: The Politics of Upheaval* (Boston: Houghton Mifflin Company, 1960); Rexford G. Tugwell, *The Democratic Roosevelt* (Baltimore: Penguin Books, 1969); and George Wolfskill and John A. Hudson, *All But the People: Franklin D. Roosevelt and His Critics, 1933–1939* (New York: Macmillan Company, 1969). David H. Bennett, *Demagogues in the Depression: American Radicals and the Union Party, 1932–1936* (New Brunswick, N.J.: Rutgers University Press, 1969), describes the campaign in which Gerald Smith participated. Robert Penn Warren's *All the King's Men* (New York: Bantam Books, Inc., 1946) is a prize-winning novel in which one of the central characters is roughly based on Long.

The Great Depression in Louisiana and the patronage battle between Long and Roosevelt have been the subjects of several published and many unpublished studies. The published studies include John Robert Moore, "The New Deal in Louisiana," in John Braeman et al., eds., *The New Deal* (Columbus, Ohio: Ohio State University Press, 1975); Roman Heleniak, "Local Reaction to the Great Depression in New Orleans, 1929–1933," *Louisiana History*, 10 (Fall 1969); and Virgil L. Mitchell, *The Civil Works Administration in Louisiana: A Study in New Deal Relief, 1933–34* (Lafayette, La.: USL History Series, 1976).

Hilda Phelps Hammond, *Let Freedom Ring* (New York: Farrar, 1936) is the only study of the anti-Long opposition written by a prominent enemy of Long. Adras Laborde's *A National Southerner: Ransdell of Louisiana* (New York: Benziger Brothers, Inc., 1951) covers the career of the senator whom Long defeated in 1930. Floyd Martin Clay, *Coozan Dudley LeBlanc: From Huey Long to Hadocal* (Gretna, La.: Pelican Publishing Company, 1974), is a study of Long's most colorful opponent.

Index

M